This book is a special treat. You will be enlightened, informed, and inspired. An astute melding of theory and practice that is grounded in reality by expert practitioners. A major contribution and a must-read for all who are committed to enhancing organizational performance.

—MICHAEL J. DOWLING, CEO, Northwell Health

A deeply wise and actionable approach for any health system looking to make improvements in safety, quality, and patient experience. The research and case studies provide a practical how-to guide for making an impact on the employee experience, and by extension, the patient experience. Absolutely essential reading.

—HEATHER BRACE, SVP and Chief People Officer,
Intermountain Healthcare

Building an engaged workforce is a journey. *The Engaged Caregiver* provides practical advice and key insights on how to develop and promote a transformational organizational culture and cultivate a caring environment for colleagues, caregivers, and patients alike.

—TRACY CHURCH, EVP and Chief Administrative Officer,
Hartford HealthCare

If you believe, as I do, that an organization is ultimately a human community, then nothing can be more important than the transformation of workplace elements—culture, experience, and quality. This book is indispensable for HR leaders looking to cultivate an adaptive approach toward executing their strategies.

—JIM DUNN, PHD, EVP and System CHRO, Atrium Health

The Engaged Caregiver identifies the critical steps that leaders need to take to make the engagement of those who care for our patients the highest strategic priority. It also illuminates how to begin developing effective leadership now and for the future. Much food not only for thought but for action.

—DEB HICKS, SVP and Chief People and Culture Officer,
Dana-Farber Cancer Institute

At long last, a book that makes the compelling case of connecting workforce culture and engagement to patient-centered outcomes. Through detailed stories and strategies, the authors state what so many of us miss: healthcare systems operate most effectively when the entire workforce is engaged, inclusive, and caring. *The Engaged Caregiver* is an invaluable resource, whether your healthcare system already has a high-performing culture or is working to achieve that goal.

—DANI MONROE, Chief Diversity, Inclusion,
and Equity Officer, Partners HealthCare,
and author of *Untapped Talent*

The healthcare industry is behind other industries in the critical area of employee engagement and culture, but it is rapidly catching up. *The Engaged Caregiver* should be read by every healthcare organization leader because it digs deep into the causes and challenges of a disengaged workforce while laying out a comprehensive and detailed plan to improve engagement and culture and, as a consequence of that, the employee experience. That, in turn, can mobilize the entire organization to improve the patient experience as a whole.

—ALFREDO CABRERA, System SVP and CHRO,
Montefiore Medical Center

This book highlights why we as healthcare leaders need to focus on the overall experience, care, and well-being of our caregivers. Engaging, practical, and well-written, *The Engaged Caregiver* is a crucial resource that addresses one of healthcare's most pressing issues.

—LINDA MCHUGH, CHRO, Cleveland Clinic

Loaded with insights for healthcare leaders interested in building a highly engaged, performance-driven workforce, *The Engaged Caregiver* offers real-world examples and strategies that highlight the critical role an engaged workforce plays in driving safety, quality, and improved patient experience.

—REGGIE STOVER, Senior Executive and CHRO,
Boston Children's Hospital

Despite increasing challenges and growing complexity in healthcare, this book makes it clear that this is a people industry and people are an organization's greatest asset. The authors offer thoughtful, inclusive, and transformative concepts and tools to empower leaders to develop critical strategies and take action. Together, these concepts will enable any organization to cultivate and sustain a highly engaged workforce capable of delivering truly exceptional care.

—JOSEPH MOSCOLA, SVP and Chief People Officer,
Northwell Health

THE
ENGAGED
CAREGIVER

THE
ENGAGED
CAREGIVER

HOW TO BUILD A
PERFORMANCE-DRIVEN
WORKFORCE TO
REDUCE BURNOUT
& TRANSFORM CARE

EDITED BY

JOSEPH CABRAL · THOMAS H. LEE, MD · MARTIN WRIGHT

Mc
Graw
Hill

New York Chicago San Francisco Athens London Madrid
Mexico City Milan New Delhi Singapore Sydney Toronto

1 2 3 4 5 6 7 8 9   LCR   24 23 22 21 20 19

ISBN   978-1-260-46129-9
MHID   1-260-46129-7

e-ISBN   978-1-260-46130-5
e-MHID   1-260-46130-0

Library of Congress Cataloging-in-Publication Data

Names: Cabral, Joseph, editor.
Title: The engaged caregiver : how to build a performance-driven workforce
    to reduce burnout and transform care / edited by Joseph Cabral, Thomas H.
    Lee, MD, and Martin Wright.
Description: New York, New York : McGraw-Hill, [2020] | Includes
    bibliographical references and index.
Identifiers: LCCN 2019034934 (print) | LCCN 2019034935 (ebook) | ISBN
    9781260461299 | ISBN 9781260461305 (e-ISBN)
Subjects: LCSH: Medical personnel—Job stress. | Medical personnel—
    Personnel management. | Caregivers—Job stress. | Burnout (Psychology)
Classification: LCC RA410.7 .E54 2020 (print) | LCC RA410.7 (ebook) |
    DDC 362.11068/3—dc23
LC record available at https://lccn.loc.gov/2019034934
LC ebook record available at https://lccn.loc.gov/2019034935

To the millions of caregivers—physicians, nurses,

and employees—who commit themselves

every day to reducing patient suffering

Contents

Foreword

Thomas H. Lee, MD, MSc

IN MEDICINE, WHEN we ignore root causes, we often wind up treating symptoms rather than the underlying disease. We might treat a fever with aspirin, leaving untouched the infection causing it. We might prescribe sedatives to relieve anxiety, failing to address the depression that is ultimately causing distress.

In healthcare management, many leaders and managers worry about issues such as clinician burnout or financial performance. But if healthcare faced no financial challenges, and if nobody in your workforce complained of burnout, would everything suddenly be "just fine"? I don't think so. We would still have important work to do to make healthcare safer, more reliable technically, more coordinated, and more compassionate. And we would still need to ensure that doctors, nurses, and other personnel loved their work, were ready to go the extra mile for their patients, and took pride in improving care.

So here is the good news. If you look closely, you find that a common root cause underlies healthcare's financial and burnout challenges: caregiver disengagement. We desperately need caregivers who love their work and are dedicated to doing their very best on the job. When such enthusiasm fails to materialize, healthcare suffers across the board. Caregiver engagement certainly doesn't guarantee high quality and business success, but we stand little chance of achieving our goals without it.

Some organizations have excelled in a single dimension of performance while maintaining low engagement levels. For example, some hospitals have focused intensely on safety—something my colleagues and I are all for—while ignoring engagement. "All we are asking you to do," they tell their workforces, "is to focus on hand hygiene and bloodstream infection reduction. Get patients out the door as quickly as possible without harming them." This is an incomplete approach. A goal of Zero Harm is just the beginning of improvement efforts—a path toward creating a culture that is reliably excellent on other aspects of care that matter to patients and caregivers.

Which brings me to a second piece of good news: we are now coming to understand how to create High Reliability cultures in which engaged caregivers are the norm, not the exception, and which promote a variety of goals, including safety and quality. More than at any time in the past:

- We know how to measure engagement.

- We understand engagement's relationship to burnout and to activation and decompression among caregivers, the key elements that affect their resilience.

- We understand how to identify caregivers who are most open to becoming engaged, and then how to welcome them in, so that organizational values resonate and become imprinted on them.

- We understand the critical role played by leaders and middle management.

- We have a more sophisticated understanding of our workforces, including the special issues faced by nurses and physicians.

- We better understand the nature of culture and how to change it.

Although work certainly remains to be done in all these areas, we've accomplished so much, to the point where it would be a mistake to think of "the engaged caregiver" as merely a rhetorical flourish. At many organizations today, it has become both an operational imperative and a competitive advantage. This book introduces you to some of these organizations, passing along the state of the art, and showing you how to cultivate and support engaged caregivers in your hospital or health system. Use it to guide and inspire you as you take what I hope will be an enriching journey, not just for you but for your caregivers and, most importantly, for your patients.

Acknowledgments

FOR MORE THAN 30 years, Press Ganey has dedicated itself to reducing patient suffering by helping improve the safety, quality, and experience of care. To perform this work, we rely every day on the great dedication, passion, and enthusiasm of our 1,200 associates, for which we're immeasurably grateful. We also benefit from the outstanding leadership of Pat Ryan, our executive chair, and Joe Greskoviak, our CEO and president, both of whom live our values and challenge us to help our partners consistently meet patients' and caregivers' needs. Thank you, Pat and Joe, for the inspiration you bring.

When we first proposed this book to Patricia Cmielewski, Press Ganey's chief administrative officer, she instantly recognized the value it would have for our industry. Thank you, Patti, for always providing such great inspiration and support for our thought leadership projects. Likewise, this book would not exist without the efforts of Gregg DiPietro, Press Ganey's senior vice president of marketing, who shepherded the book through the publication process. Thank you, Gregg!

The editors would also like to recognize each of the chapter authors for their commitment to the project. Somehow, each of these experts found a bit of extra time in their already full days to work on this—getting up a little earlier, going to bed a little later, and reading and writing between meetings. Thank you to Matt Turner, who consistently accepts every challenge presented to him with grace and tenacity; to Ingrid Summers, who challenges us to think differently in all aspects of our work; to Lynn Ehrmantraut, whose dedication to improving patient and employee experiences has defined her incredible career; to Shannon Vincent, who plays a huge role in shaping the strategy and client deliverables for Press Ganey's Workforce Solutions group; to Eric Heckerson, who brings modern adult-learning insights to our team; to Brad Pollins, who has reshaped the way we think about leadership development; to Kristopher Morgan, who prioritizes the science of our work to ensure reliability and validity for our clients; to Stephanie Weimer, who travels tirelessly to provide insights and recommendations to our clients on how to transform their cultures; and to Dave Shinsel, who drives our clients and our people to new heights with his coaching and leadership.

We also wish to recognize and thank Christy Dempsey and Mary Jo Assi, whose efforts are shaping nursing practice and culture around the world. Thank you to Chrissy Daniels, who challenges us to consider all points along the care continuum; and to Deirdre Mylod for developing a framework that helps us address burnout, one of the biggest challenges in healthcare today. Thank you to Craig Clapper and Steve Kreiser, safety experts who are saving countless lives by helping organizations move closer to Zero Harm. Finally, thank you to Rachel Biblow for helping healthcare leaders think holistically, break down silos, and truly transform healthcare.

In addition, we wish to acknowledge the following individuals and organizations for graciously sharing their time, stories, experiences, and insights: Advocate Aurora Health; Cleveland Clinic;

Hartford HealthCare; Inspira Health; Intermountain Healthcare; Dr. Thomas Howell and Mayo Clinic; MultiCare Health System; Dr. Patrick J. Cawley and MUSC Health; Nationwide Children's Hospital; Northwell Health; Novant Health; Dr. Virginia Casey and OrthoCarolina; OSF HealthCare; Dani Monroe and Partners HealthCare; Providence St. Joseph Health; Royal Bank of Canada; Angelique Richard and Rush University Medical Center; Salem Health; Seattle Children's Hospital; Sentara Healthcare; Tidelands Health; Janet L. Christie and UF Health Shands; University of Tennessee Medical Center; Julie Kennedy Oehlert and Vidant Health; Washington Health System; and Yale New Haven Health System.

We were able to complete this project because of the hard work and direction provided by Diana Mahoney, director of content strategy, and Audrey Doyle, senior editorial manager, both of Press Ganey. Diana curates our thought leadership and ensures that everything we do is compelling, connected, and readable. As a talented writer who is passionately committed to our mission, Audrey performed the "heavy lifting" on this project, helping less experienced authors find their voice and more experienced authors tighten their messages. Both Diana and Audrey ensured that this project moved forward and stayed on deadline.

This is the third book project we've completed with our editor, Seth Schulman, whom we now nearly consider a member of the Press Ganey family. Seth and his colleague, Rachel Gostenhofer, masterfully knit the component parts of this book together to ensure that the final narrative was clear, cohesive, and powerful. Finally, we wish to acknowledge Casey Ebro, executive editor at McGraw-Hill. By recognizing the importance of this project as well as previous ones, she has helped advance our mission to improve healthcare. Thank you, Casey!

Introduction

Martin Wright

> *An engaged and resilient workforce is essential for achieving robust safety, quality, and patient experience outcomes. To catalyze high performance, healthcare organizations must prioritize workforce engagement, accelerating improvement, creating alignment, and fostering an engaged culture.*

THE HIGH-PERFORMING EXECUTIVE team of a large health system had gathered for its organization's annual strategy retreat. Although the organization was doing well, passions sometimes ran high on the team, leading to heated debates and disagreements. The decision-making process was sometimes opaque, and behind-the-scenes maneuvering often prevented true collaboration. Wishing to cultivate greater trust among team members, strengthen relationships, and improve communication, organizers of the retreat had devised a new team-building activity. They had asked attendees to each bring a significant personal item and discuss its meaning and value with the group. Some leaders brushed off the exercise, bringing mundane objects whose superficial meanings allowed for little personal transparency or vulnerability. But the organization's chief operating officer (COO) brought a memorable object, attached to an even more memorable story.

Some in the organization perceived this COO as aloof, disconnected from the organization's mission, and unwilling to listen. Those who knew her and worked closely with her respected her work, appreciated her grasp of operations, and admired her understanding of the organization, even when they disagreed with her. When asked to discuss her item, the COO displayed a gold trophy depicting a basketball player. Many in the room, having seen the trophy on her desk at work, had assumed it belonged to her son, but in fact it was her older brother's from when he was a kid. About a decade earlier, the COO explained, her brother had passed away after a bout with cancer. Although he had been sick for a few years, the end had come suddenly and taken the family by surprise. "I had been busy at the time building my career," the COO said, "and I hadn't been paying as much attention to him as I should have. He was always the strong one, the star athlete. Even when he got sick, it didn't seem like he needed me much. But in a journal of his that we found, he wrote that he felt so lonely because of his illness, cut off from the rest of the world. If I had been more sensitive and a better sister, maybe he wouldn't have felt that way." She was crying; everyone was. The COO went on to describe how her brother lives on in her memory—that she does her work out of deference to him. "It's because of him that I'm passionate about healthcare," the COO said, "and that I do everything in my power to advance this organization's mission each and every day."[1]

The group was stunned. Thanks to this one brief story, they now understood what drove one of their close colleagues, what ignited her passion. Further, they appreciated how a professional with no clinical experience or exposure to patients could remain steadfastly committed to the organization. In this instance, personal transparency led to both vulnerability and authenticity on the COO's part, binding the leadership team together around the importance of their daily work and larger mission.

We in healthcare are in the business of providing care to patients when they need it most. We need to foster authenticity and build teams in which all members understand their teammates' motivations and appreciate their contributions. Unfortunately, that often doesn't happen—not in executive suites, and not among the rank and file. Most executive teams remain guarded, formal, and even somewhat aloof, disconnected from their passion and purpose. They also don't pay close attention to whether *others* in the organization are pursuing work in passionate, soulful ways, nor do they embrace culture as a driving force for change. No surprise that our workforces are not nearly as engaged and activated as they might be, as committed to the organization's mission, and as capable of delivering on our basic promise of providing safe, high-quality, patient-centered care.

According to data that Press Ganey collected from across the United States, engagement has declined since 2016 for nearly 1.6 million healthcare workers. Millennials, who comprise our workforce's largest generational group, were the least engaged, as were registered nurses, our workforce's largest employee segment.[2] As engagement wanes, safety, quality, and experience outcomes also suffer. In a recent study, organizations in the top quartile on both employee and physician engagement saw better safety and clinical quality outcomes than those in the bottom quartile, as well as shorter lengths of stay, fewer readmissions, and stronger performance across patient experience measures.[3] Engagement also influences an organization's financial health. The same study found that organizations in the top quartile for engagement had higher net margins and lower spending for patient readmissions.[4]

But engagement and the inspiring of resilient, passionate care teams is just one of several interconnected talent management goals that healthcare organizations typically pursue. Leaders also wish to attract and retain top talent, hire better people faster, reduce onboarding time, and improve employee longevity by increasing their effectiveness. Leaders wish to manage the shifting workforce demographics and meet the needs and expectations of each workforce segment, with an eye toward work's future evolution. Leaders wish to develop managers who provide career opportunities, helpful performance feedback, and an effective work environment for their teams. Finally, leaders wish to maximize patient, workforce, *and* business outcomes to ensure the organization's long-term success.

Most organizations are finding these goals increasingly elusive. In a period of near-zero unemployment, organizations struggle to find the right type and number of candidates,[5] and also to keep that talent once they find it. Healthcare employee turnover rates hover at 17 percent nationally and continue to rise. Attrition among new nurses is currently about 17.5 percent the first year, increasing to 33.5 percent and 43 percent during the second and third years, respectively. Since professional healthcare roles are highly skilled, turnover has a wide-ranging impact, affecting patient care, healthcare culture, and organizational finances.[6] Burnout is also an issue, *impairing professionals' ability to meet job demands and adversely influencing the safety and quality of patient care.*[7] Physician burnout rates vary from 40 to 78 percent, depending on the study and medical specialty, and burnout among nurses runs as high as 60 percent.[8]

Solving these and related problems is not easy. Leaders seeking to form comprehensive talent management strategies often feel stymied by generational differences and other forms of diversity, which seem to require more customized approaches. And yet, we must make progress—the health of our patients and of our organizations depends on it. The answer is to double down on engagement and culture. Leaders must take these imperatives far more seriously than they have to date. They must elevate their work in this area and align themselves strategically around culture-shaping factors proven to drive change. They must create welcoming contexts in which people can bring their best selves to work and feel deeply committed to the organization's mission. Only then will employees feel inspired to do their best on the job each day. Only then will they provide the highest quality, most affordable care.

Understanding Culture and Engagement

In intensifying their commitment to enhancing culture and engagement, leaders must understand these concepts and the relationship between them in a precise way. Many leaders think of engagement as a tactical concept confined to data collection. It's a score from the most recent employee survey, they assume, or the action plans associated with those findings. At worst, some leaders simplistically conflate engagement with providing a "happy" place to work—what we call the "pizza party" mentality.

True engagement doesn't center on personal happiness or "satisfaction," nor does it center on surveys. Satisfaction contributes to engagement, but the latter is a much broader and deeper concept. Employees might feel satisfied when they enjoy their work, when they feel appreciated and respected, and when they maintain strong relationships with their coworkers and with managers. But employees become truly engaged when they forge a strong *emotional* bond with the organization they are a part of, taking pride in what they do and speaking favorably about their employer to friends and family. Ask people in healthcare why they chose their profession, and they will often describe a personal passion or mission similar to the one articulated by the COO at the beginning of this Introduction. This calling gives rise to a strong emotional bond not just with the caregiver's organization, but with the profession in general, immediately elevating the meaning of "engagement" throughout the industry.

Because engaged employees feel so emotionally connected, they tend to make an extra effort on the job—like the caregiver who takes on an extra shift for a coworker when the unit is short-staffed or when a colleague must call out unexpectedly to help a sick child. Engaged employees also co-own their engagement with the team or organization. Rather than waiting for leaders or direct supervisors to create optimal work conditions, they take the initiative to improve the environment in support of the organization's own goals. Finally, engaged employees commit to improving themselves, developing their skills and abilities so they can better serve the organization's mission.

We can think of culture, meanwhile, as a set of beliefs and values shared by members within a given group as well as by outsiders who interact with the group. Culture in this sense forms the foundation of effective "people strategies," propelling organizations forward toward achieving their missions and visions. And yet, culture is inherently mutable. If leaders don't intentionally address it, it can evolve in unproductive ways. Organizations must thus *design* culture, with leaders carefully considering how they want caregivers to think, feel, and act when at work, and how those thoughts, feelings, and actions support the organization's overall goals. An important first step is to regard chief human resources officers (CHROs) as culture *creators*, not merely keepers or monitors of the culture, as they've traditionally been. These leaders must drive strategy and development, taking the organizational effort beyond annual employee satisfaction surveys, action plans, and traditional human resources operations.

At Press Ganey, we conceive of engagement as a *barometer* or early indicator of cultural changes. When engagement increases, the culture is improving. A shared sense of purpose is taking root and flourishing, and people feel inspired and start to lean into their work. Teams are also beginning to mesh and operate together more effectively. As engagement decreases, the underlying culture is weakening. Individuals are becoming more isolated, and teams are fragmenting.

Leaders who understand this relationship can intervene when engagement scores decline. One high-performing organization with whom we've long partnered has faithfully measured employee engagement. One year, amid significant leadership and cultural changes as well as multiple acquisitions, the system's survey revealed scores that were unusually low in key areas. Digging into the data, the chief executive officer (CEO) and CHRO identified three variables—perceptions of benefits, the caregivers' perceptions of their transparency, and the trust caregivers had in leaders—that were negatively influencing caregivers' experiences. The CEO and CHRO quickly developed an improvement strategy to target these variables. Their efforts preempted possible damage to the organization's existing culture and kept the organization on track to reaching its overarching goals.

Who Owns Engagement?

It's significant that both the CEO and the CHRO at this organization took responsibility for monitoring engagement levels. Traditionally, human resources has owned engagement, but as leading-edge organizations have found, that notion is woefully outdated and corrosive of organizational culture. Engagement must be an organization-wide imperative, given the same attention, rigor, and buy-in as safety, quality, and finance. Starting at the board level, health system leaders must promote and catalyze an engaged culture. Through executive sponsorship of engagement efforts, visible leadership to reinforce culture, and consistent role modeling of engagement-building behaviors, leaders can cultivate an atmosphere of trust and mutual respect—the foundations of a robust, healthy culture. Leaders must also support the culture vocally, communicating the organization's mission, vision, and values consistently. They must craft a supportive infrastructure that develops high-performing teams and leaders capable of achieving and sustaining high performance. Finally, by eliminating workforce "cancers" like bullying and incivility as part of an interconnected strategy, leaders can also elevate engagement from a once-a-year cultural measurement to a critical driver of business outcomes.

Leaders at some organizations are focusing on enhancing engagement and culture. New York–based Northwell Health, one of the nation's largest integrated health systems, began its cultural transformation when engagement rankings fell below the 50th percentile in Press Ganey's engagement database. The health system's CEO, Michael Dowling, took decisive action, declaring that the organization would become a "best place to work in healthcare." With support from the leadership team, Northwell Health explicitly defined engagement as a strategic imperative, not just an HR project. That meant holding quarterly People Strategy meetings with department leadership, performing annual talent reviews, and conducting leadership assessments for all director-level leaders and higher to determine mismatches and learning opportunities. In 2016, Northwell, then known as North Shore Long Island Jewish Health System, launched a broad rebranding campaign. Along with its name change, the organization publicly recommitted to improving employee engagement, wellness, and communication. Recognizing engagement as a driving force of other outcomes, leaders aspired to rank in the 90th percentile for both employee engagement and patient experience.

Northwell committed to a regular cadence of engagement and patient experience surveying, including a full engagement survey annually and mid-year pulse surveys across the continuum of care. Northwell forged this survey strategy to ensure transparency. Leader rounding on staff became a requirement across Northwell Health, and senior leaders communicated regularly about the value of the survey process, the results of the surveys, and the organization's response to the results. These leaders recognized successes and also required 90-day engagement action plans when the data identified leaders and teams in need of improvement. The organization created an employee telephone app that facilitated instant and consistent communication, and a value proposition called "Made for This" that articulated the employee commitment to patient care.

While still striving to reach top decile performance, Northwell Health has achieved back-to-back annual percentile rankings in the 80th percentile or higher in the Press Ganey database. Although many factors have contributed to Northwell's success, Michael Dowling's vocal and visible commitment as well as that of his team proved decisive. As leaders, we cast a long shadow on those we serve—we must never underestimate our impact. As of this writing in 2019, Dowling still attends new-hire orientation each week, and he believes his most important role as CEO is his continued investment in the system's nearly 70,000 associates. "Give them your time, answers, ears, attention, perspective, and, perhaps every now and then, selfies," he says. "Healthcare has its challenges, but nothing gets done without teams of people. Working in this profession is not a job—it's a privilege and responsibility."[9]

Aligning the Organization Around Culture and Engagement

Beyond a sustained commitment from leaders, organizations can quicken progress on culture and engagement if they align the organization behind improvement goals. Fundamentally, this requires that leaders articulate a shared mission around which all team members can rally, what we refer to as a True North. In healthcare, this guiding point illuminates the organization's path to patient-centered care in the face of changing metrics, measures, and government requirements. Maintaining a single, clearly articulated focus helps caregivers stay the course in times of fear and uncertainty.

Organizations differ in how they frame their True North guidepost. Some commit to Zero Harm, prioritizing safety as driving overall patient experience. At these organizations, caregivers commit to eliminating preventable harm by improving the way systems, processes, and people collaborate. Other organizations, such as Cleveland Clinic, have adopted a patient-centric mentality as their True North. In 2004, shortly after Dr. Delos "Toby" Cosgrove became CEO of the Ohio-based nonprofit academic medical center, he introduced the motto of "patients first" to remind caregivers that leaders must first consider what is best for the patient when making any organizational decision. Dr. Cosgrove chose this motto because it brought the organization back to its roots. As founding member William E. Lower declared, "The patient is the most important person in the organization."[10]

With a True North in place, organizations must then identify the shared values they want all caregivers to embody and project. Aligned with the True North guidepost, these values amount to a pact that employees accept and that in turn shapes how teams operate to achieve desired outcomes. Leaders should empower a select, representative group of individuals within the organization to choose these values, and they should confirm that the values chosen connect to the organization's desired culture. Going forward, these values should underlie all aspects of the organizational culture and engagement efforts.

Many organizations flounder because they don't incorporate values into their overall strategy. They might hold a senior leadership retreat off-site at a beautiful resort, discussing the organization's mission and goals and how they will be achieved. Leaders then create a set of values they believe represents the organization well, plan a grand rollout of the new values, and expect everyone in the organization to live those values every day. Unfortunately, many in the organization don't understand these values, nor do they comprehend leaders' rationales for selecting them. Organizations can't develop and execute on a mission statement and values with just placards, posters, email signatures, and lapel pins. Such efforts might "speak" to some caregivers, but they have little impact on others.

One proverb holds that we must communicate in seven ways, seven times, for individuals to completely internalize information. When it comes to culture and engagement, seven might not be enough. Leaders must relentlessly communicate values, explaining how they relate to the daily work of caring for patients, and clarifying how caregivers must express values on the job in their words and actions. Just as patients can choose where to receive care, so too can employees determine where they work and practice. Setting clear expectations and establishing guidelines for working together to provide the best care for patients creates an environment where everyone feels recognized and valued.

To keep employees focused on standards of behavior, leading-edge organizations communicate their expectations on an ongoing basis. Leaders across the enterprise receive training in the desired behaviors, beginning with the executive leadership team. While the content of behavioral training might not be new to the executive team, their participation showcases their commitment and sets the tone for the rest of the organization. After executive training, all people leaders and then all caregivers should undergo training. When caregivers see the organization investing time and resources into this effort, they'll feel more optimistic about the effort's sustainability. Organizations should also incorporate the standards of behavior into new-hire orientation and onboarding efforts. If they do, additional training won't be necessary, since new hires will experience the desired behaviors on a day-to-day basis and through frequent communication "booster shots" from leaders.

To ensure that leaders and staff actually apply standards of behaviors to their daily activities, leaders can create daily standard work that aligns with the expected behaviors, localizing the effort and thus creating a stickier connection for caregivers. Leaders should conduct a rapid improvement event with their teams to grasp the department's current state as it relates to service behaviors; define the ideal state and how the department might adopt the behaviors in its day-to-day activities; and identify leading, real-time, and lagging indicators that can help the team members understand the long-term impact of this work on both staff and patients. Finally, to ensure the successful implementation of these service behaviors, the organization should create a clear, consistent, leader-driven communication plan. The 5 Ps Method of communication described in Chapter 4 is an effective tool for ensuring clarity and authenticity of messaging.

How to Use This Book

The elements we've sketched out here are just the beginning of what healthcare organizations must do to build strong cultures and create highly engaged workforces. The chapters that follow present a much more detailed and holistic approach. Based on over 20 years of insights gathered from our measurement and improvement work in healthcare as well as the hands-on experience of our panel of expert authors, we present a framework for building a robust culture and accelerating improvement to support the delivery of safe, high-quality, patient-centered care. Our chapters provide a comprehensive approach to talent management and can serve as an everyday reference for leaders seeking to enhance the people management and leadership work already underway in their organizations.

Chapter 1 explores the differences between transactional human resources management and the more contemporary view of strategic talent management. These differences are considerable, and a strategic approach allows human resources to harness the power of culture, transform the organization, and enhance performance. In **Chapter 2**, we explore diversity, equity, and inclusion. If we are to have a culture that truly supports patient care, we must ensure that we fully respect everyone in our workforce. **Chapter 3** lays out a comprehensive strategy for building engagement. Whether your organization is implementing an engagement strategy for the first time or you are a seasoned professional, the insights in this chapter will provide the broad guidance you need to achieve your engagement goals.

Great leaders helm great healthcare organizations, and our investment in talent development starts with leadership development, the topic of **Chapter 4**. Healthcare organizations often promote great clinicians into leadership roles without investing the resources necessary to turn these great clinicians into great leaders. In this chapter, we discuss a framework for developing leader competencies to support cultural enrichment.

For readers interested in understanding measurement and engagement science more deeply, **Chapter 5** covers measure development, testing, and validation, and **Chapter 6** illuminates how to put the data to work. Data and insights provide a critical improvement path when collected using optimal measurement tools. Leaders must understand how caregivers perceive the entire workplace environment, including perceptions of safety culture, teamwork, managers, resilience levels among individuals and their teams, and the organization as a whole. Understanding how to leverage the right data in a way that makes sense and helps managers and leaders focus on what is important allows for effective execution on the strategy.

Chapter 7 focuses on the work environment that nurses experience. Two nurse leaders with extensive experience in research and practice explore how important it is to understand nurses' unique needs and optimize engagement efforts accordingly. **Chapter 8** is devoted to physician engagement strategy. Physicians play an instrumental role in leading culture, and this chapter explores the key elements that engage this critical stakeholder group.

Next, we move on to some important challenges that prevent healthcare workforces from bringing their best selves to work. **Chapter 9** tackles professional burnout, introducing a practical approach to understanding, measuring, and coping with this unfortunate and persistent problem. **Chapter 10** delves more systematically into workforce safety. When caregivers perceive the safety of patients and employees as an organizational priority, they strive to make the environment safer, and their engagement rises in due course. In this chapter, our safety experts explain how safety and engagement create a virtuous cycle to accelerate improvement.

In **Chapter 11**, we coalesce many strands of this book into a discussion of the patient experience. Culture and engagement ultimately matter because they allow us to improve how we care for patients. As we argue in this chapter, transforming our organizations so they can better deliver safe, high-quality, patient-centered care requires that leaders adopt an integrated strategy rooted in engagement and culture. This chapter presents a framework for advancing the patient experience, introducing 10 critical steps for execution that can ensure progress in this area.

Although leaders at healthcare organizations have not traditionally grappled with workforce culture and engagement, they can no longer refrain from doing so. At a time when other industries are deploying robots to get work done, healthcare is still a people industry and becoming more so every day. In 2017, our industry became the largest source of jobs in the country, eclipsing manufacturing and retail sectors to account for nearly 20 percent of the labor force. Over the next five years, healthcare will add over two million more jobs.[11] With employees factoring ever more prominently into organizations' success, leaders will have to attend to employee needs far better than they have in the past. Although many leaders might struggle today to attract, retain, and engage employees, we can transform our organizations into places where every employee feels the kind of deep, emotional connection to their work that the COO described at the beginning of this Introduction does. Let us hope that we do. Our future—and our ability to provide safe, compassionate, high-quality care to patients—depends on it.

IN SUM

- Healthcare organizations must prioritize the design and deployment of a culture of engagement in order to accelerate improvement.
- Engagement acts as a barometer for culture, providing leading indicators of what's working well and where improvement opportunities might exist.
- Culture change happens when leadership visibly and vocally commits to it as a strategic priority; when the organization aligns around a True North; and when standards of behavior are developed, communicated, and universally inculcated.
- A culture of engagement is the engine that drives safety, quality, and patient experience outcomes.

THE
ENGAGED
CAREGIVER

The Critical Importance of Strategic Talent Management

Joseph Cabral, MS, and Matt Turner, MA

> *Most healthcare organizations approach workforce engagement and talent management tactically; so, they are ill-prepared for coming changes in technology, demographics, and mode of care delivery. Leading organizations position themselves better by investing strategically in their culture, practices, and processes.*

As Bruce Bailey, president and CEO of Tidelands Health, drove to work during the predawn hours of September 11, 2018, he felt a mix of concern and confidence. He and his executive team had been tracking the development of Hurricane Florence over the previous two days. The storm seemed poised to hit their community hard and to confront the organization with a host of unknown challenges. Still, Bailey felt confident because his team had done its homework, and his employees were highly engaged.

As he pulled into his facility's parking lot, Gayle Resetar, the system's chief operating officer (COO), was already on-site, and the entire command center was a whirlwind of activity. Live television broadcasts showed Florence, a Category 4 hurricane, now on track for a direct hit. Tidelands Health needed to comply with a state order and evacuate the system's patients and the majority of its staff, and do it safely. Still, the team's huddle that morning was almost unnecessary—leaders knew that frontline caregivers were up to the challenge. They had trained for situations such as this, and the organizational processes were firmly in place. The team made the decision: it was go time.

Hospitals and healthcare systems across the United States face something like an approaching hurricane when it comes to talent management, thanks to changes in technology, demographics, and care delivery models. We don't know where these looming threats will exert their greatest impacts, so preparation and planning are critical. While healthcare's traditional values of empathy, service, and teamwork should still guide our industry, we must proactively reorient our cultures to embrace the adaptability, innovation, and agility that will prove decisive for individual, team, and organizational success.

Tidelands Health and other leading organizations are already doing so by adjusting their talent management strategies. These organizations understand that leaders bear responsibility for developing a highly engaged workforce, embedding an effective talent management strategy into the culture, and reinforcing that strategy in daily operations. This chapter considers some of the megatrends confronting healthcare and draws from organizations like Tidelands Health to propose solutions. Rather than provide an exhaustive inventory of tools, tactics, and how-to approaches, we profile several industry exemplars, focusing on their key practices in the core areas of leadership, recruiting, talent selection, onboarding, and retention.

Prepare for Tomorrow, Today

We can think of strategic talent management as "an integrated set of processes, programs, and cultural norms in an organization designed and implemented to attract, develop, deploy, and retain talent to achieve strategic objectives and meet future business needs."[1] While this concept was first popularized in the late 1990s,[2] and a model for strategic talent management began crystallizing over the past three decades, organizations still vary in how they've adopted and implemented these practices. Many view talent management not as a set of "cultural norms" keyed to both present and future needs, but merely as a set of tactical processes, practices, and transactions designed to fill open positions and minimize turnover. Such organizations treat talent management much like accountants view cash flow. Successful talent management means that credits slightly outnumber debits; that vacancies, turnover, and days to fill remain slightly below industry benchmarks; that training offerings, internal promotions, and staffing ratios nominally exceed industry benchmarks; and that the pipeline or pool of available talent is reasonably full, managed, and engaged to meet immediate business needs.

Organizations displaying this transactional mind-set typically possess a strong cultural norm of egalitarianism. Nearly all employees and managers are rated as "exceeding" or "far exceeding" expectations on annual performance reviews, despite frequent and serious safety events. Everyone receives an incremental pay raise, no matter their contribution. Talent management is classified as a problem for human resources to solve and manage, and proposed solutions are often reactive. In short, under the transactional approach, strategic talent management is not very "strategic" at all.

Leading organizations view talent management differently and work diligently to optimize every stage of the talent management life cycle (Table 1.1). Such organizations view talent management as a business imperative, a mechanism that aligns the enterprise around the delivery of value at the critical intersection of safety, quality, and patient-centricity. These organizations also view talent management as more than a set of processes, practices, or key performance indicators (KPIs), but an array of cultural norms. Career growth, for example, is one of several key differentiators between Press Ganey's top decile clients and the broader healthcare industry.[3] Top decile clients harbor an explicit cultural norm related to a "growth mindset."[4] Leaders, managers, and employees understand personal growth not just as an individual aspiration, but as a practice that talent management processes must augment and that the organizations' leadership practices must reinforce.

Table 1.1   Transactional Versus Strategic Talent Management

Transactional	Strategic
From	To
Focus on processes and practices	A strategic business imperative
Address immediate needs	Positioned to address future needs
Static and cumbersome processes	Adaptive and agile processes
Owned by human resources	Championed by HR but owned by leadership
Annual evaluation	Ongoing assessment

Within high-performing organizations, furthermore, the concept of differentiation becomes a cherished cultural norm. Just as patients have individual needs, aspirations, and expectations, so do employees. High-performing organizations establish management practices that not only foster diversity, inclusion, and equity but ensure that each employee and physician possesses the necessary job fit, psychological safety, and clarity of purpose required to become fully activated and engaged. Northwell Health's CEO, Michael Dowling, believes that he "owns the leadership gene pool" of the roughly 70,000-person organization. In pursuing their goal of becoming an employer of choice as well as a High Reliability Organization, Dowling and chief people officer Joseph Moscola hold formal quarterly reviews of their leadership talent to ensure that the overall culture is advancing and variations in leadership are declining. Ultimately, leading organizations understand that it rests squarely on the shoulders of management and leadership to deliver an effective talent management strategy and ensure that daily operations imbue, shape, grow, and reinforce culture.

Mind the Megatrends

In the years ahead, organizations will feel increased pressure to adopt a strategic approach to talent management. A review of the available literature suggests that three principal megatrends—changes in clinical and operational technologies, increasing healthcare demand, and shifting care delivery models—will have the most pronounced impacts on talent management, rendering day-to-day management more complex and placing new strains on physicians, managers, and employees. Because these trends are poised to accelerate rapidly, organizations must adapt talent management strategies now. If they don't, they risk losing the war for talent, market share, and profitability.

While some maintain that technologies such as artificial intelligence (AI) can address a wide variety of inefficiencies at the root of healthcare's decades-long productivity decline,[5] they also disrupt traditional job design and talent management. Robotics, cognitive automation, full AI, and other leading technologies will advance beyond the repetitive, rule-based tasks they perform today and become more sophisticated, judgment-based, predictive, and self-adaptive. Registration, bed management, security, billing/finance, dispatch, and medical coding all already benefit from technologies that automate or audit routine tasks, allowing individuals in these roles to focus on improving service and solving higher-order problems. While the impact of technological advancement on specific roles and work activities is difficult to predict, some experts contend that automation will impact approximately half of all healthcare roles in the next decade.[6] Existing talent management strategies must evolve in turn. Instead of defining tasks and subtasks for individual roles, and dividing and allocating work activities between humans and their technological counterparts, these strategies must focus on broader job *categories* and *families*, recognizing that entire classes of jobs will change thanks to AI.

A confluence of factors related to the graying of America will also impact healthcare, causing demand to soar in the coming decades while raising the prospect of a looming talent shortage[7] that is only partially mitigated by technology.[8] Understanding the projected demand for particular skills and services only addresses part of the problem. We must also consider the projected supply of talent along with the impact that technology will have on role requirements. While many organizations conduct in-depth studies to understand what drives nursing retention within their market, leading organizations look at roles beyond nursing, like home health aides and mission-critical information technology roles, to ensure that they are well-prepared to handle future clinical and business demands. Along with the projected labor market challenges, employees themselves bring different expectations and belief systems to the workplace. In particular, they increasingly expect their experiences at work to approximate their experiences at home, with ready access to information and web-based support tools that foster autonomy and informed decision-making. To attract and retain employees as well as optimize their performance, organizations will require an in-depth understanding of millennials and so-called Generation Z as well as adaptiveness and agility on the part of leaders.

The location and delivery of healthcare continues to change as well, with video calls, remote workers, health-monitoring apps, Internet of Things–connected medical devices, and telemedicine becoming more prevalent. In the future, healthcare delivery will largely comprise a variety of digitally driven touchpoints interspersed with episodic, traditional face-to-face care. As care delivery transforms, we must redesign our jobs, reconceiving job role functions, the physical location of the role itself, and the basic knowledge, skills, and abilities required to discharge each new role. Today, for instance, almost every physician practice employs a front desk registrar and a certified medical assistant (CMA) or registered nurse (RN). The registrar is often tasked with checking patients in, collecting insurance information, and performing a variety of other repetitive, rule-based tasks that will soon become automated. Similarly, the CMA or RN often intakes basic patient clinical information and verifies the scope of the visit. In the future, the registrar role may cease to exist, while the CMA/RN role will likely require mastery of clinical knowledge and skills as well as the ability to interface with a range of technological systems related to patients' overall health and wellness.

Evolve Your Leadership

Anticipating the changes ahead, leading-edge organizations have taken a number of steps to improve talent management. First, they've shifted leadership roles. Several organizations have created a chief clinical officer to integrate all clinical activities across the enterprise and to signal the rising imperative of cross-discipline collaboration. Similarly, organizations are beginning to replace chief human resources officers (CHROs) with chief people officers or chief talent officers. In some instances, they've rebranded the entire HR function as "talent management."

Name changes alone don't produce immediate changes in activities or performance, but they do signal a shift in thinking. No matter its name, the role of CHRO is quickly taking on the function of convener, integrator, and driver of cultural change.[9] All healthcare organizations face unrelenting pressures to reduce costs and increase efficiencies, and today many CHROs actively reduce nonessential spending on a wide range of organizational development line items within their budgets. Future-oriented CHROs make the exact opposite decisions, protecting training and development during organizational budget cuts. Aware that organizational agility and innovation require investment, leading CHROs prioritize leadership and employee development, preparing the organization for the future. They also consider the importance of mentoring programs, bright-idea campaigns, action learning projects, preceptor development, as well as budgets, staffing levels, and cultural expectations. In 2018, Myra Gregorian, chief people officer of Seattle Children's, initiated an organization-wide reflection on the basic values and operating principles of her historically exceptional organization. With the avid support of CEO Jeff Sperring and the executive team, the organization has embarked on a multiyear journey to disrupt itself and thereby ensure that it remains innovative and agile.

Leading CHROs also work to galvanize HR, safety, quality, and medical staff services to diagnose organizational issues, arrive at solutions, and hold people responsible for follow-through. Intermountain Healthcare's Heather Brace (chief people officer), Shannon Phillips (chief experience officer), and Mark Briesacher (chief physician executive) routinely convene meetings of all internal consultants within their organization for a comprehensive review of facilities and work units on KPIs like quality, safety, turnover, engagement, and resilience. This integrated support team ensures that transformational change takes place across the organization in all domains of performance.

While the CHRO's relationships with the chief nursing officer (CNO) and the chief medical officer (CMO) have always been pivotal, forward-thinking CHROs create four-way dialogues that also include the chief information officer (CIO). Such CHRO-CIO-CNO-CMO meetings ensure that discussions about future talent needs take technological advancements into account, and they also allow for agile adjustments at every step of the talent management life cycle. Leading culture requires a team mentality—dyads and triads continue to supplant the traditional silo of any one leader.

In sum, CHROs at leading organizations are changing every aspect of the talent management life cycle, pushing past traditional thinking about recruitment, onboarding, and development, subjects to which we now turn.

Rally the Recruits

A second step organizations are taking to improve talent management is to recruit the right people, and in turn, communicate the organization's employee value proposition (EVP) effectively. Organizations must create an appealing and emotionally resonant message about what makes them unique, and communicate such messaging over the phone, on social media, in traditional advertising, and in face-to-face conversations with prospects. Given how important your organization's reputation is in prospects' minds, you must invest the time, energy, and money to promote and bolster your status and perceived value in the communities you serve. Such efforts have a dual purpose: they convey that the organization is both a great place to work and an ideal place to receive care. In promoting their reputations for excellence, many organizations lead with a message and image of their best selves to attract as many skilled candidates as possible.

Of course, organizations vary in the quality and effectiveness of their messages. Leading organizations augment an artful, passionate appeal with rigorous analytics to ensure the authenticity of their EVP. Using structured inputs like exit and stay interviews, employee surveys, interview data, individual feedback from key talent (often the top 10 percent of employees in mission-critical roles), focus group feedback from highly resilient teams, and sentiment analysis, high-performing organizations seek out and synthesize a diverse set of perspectives from across the organization. As a result, their EVPs contain the necessary texture, meaning, and credibility to attract the strongest and most diverse applicant pool.

OSF Healthcare, headquartered in Peoria, Illinois, and serving a largely rural population, has developed a clear and compelling EVP based on its strong Catholic values as well as feedback it has obtained from Mission Partners, as the company calls its employees and physicians. Despite undergoing a significant, organization-wide restructuring and acquiring additional hospitals, the organization continues to draw a disproportional number of capable candidates. It also retains key talent and has seen gains in a majority of its organizational KPIs. We attribute these results, in part, to the authenticity and clarity of OSF's messaging about its values, purpose, and future. OSF employees consistently report a strong sense of "belonging" in the organization. In our era of social isolation, which some have characterized as "bowling alone,"[10] that message resonates with applicants and their employees.

Authenticity and clarity grow ever more important given the amount of data now flowing through organizations—nine times more in 2018 than 2016.[11] The presence of all of this data can help clarify purpose and enhance situational awareness at the front lines of care, but it can also overwhelm employees and lead to disparities in how well they are informed. Independent social media platforms have also arisen that allow current and former employees to voice their appreciation and concerns about current and former employers. These platforms can present a powerful counternarrative to potential applicants about the authenticity of an organization's EVP. Discrepancies in employee experience can further discredit the EVP when they go unaddressed, breeding skepticism and cynicism that can infect the larger workforce. Within the Press Ganey database, even moderately performing organizations can show differences in work-unit performance of nearly 90 percent, with some units ranking as exceptionally engaged and others as among the least engaged within our national database.

Rising internal information flows, external social media platforms, and variances in employees' work experiences will significantly shape recruitment and retention efforts in the coming years. EVP credibility will become more important given demographic shifts and the ongoing transition to more heavily blended employment models composed of full-time, part-time, contract, and gig-economy employees. Organizations that clearly describe their value to applicants and employees alike will attract and retain the strongest pools of prospective employees from which to select for open roles.

Select Top Talent

A third practice vital to making talent management more strategic is improving how the organization selects new members of its workforce. The employee selection process is dynamic, with both parties evaluating one another simultaneously. While the interviewer assesses a candidate's knowledge, skills, abilities, and overall "fit," the candidate evaluates the role, environment, manager, and team. Only if these evaluations are compatible can the hiring process proceed.

While most organizations train managers in interviewing techniques, high-performing organizations require organizational recruiters, interviewing managers, or teams (if peer interviewing is used) to articulate and reinforce the organization's EVP and overall narrative about patient-centricity. Leaders at every level are expected (and more often, inspired) to speak in specific terms about their culture, emphasizing the value of teamwork, the pre-eminence of patient safety, and the importance of learning and adaptability. Leaders and employees at these organizations know the headlines, "talking points," and cultural "narrative," helping applicants to see themselves either "fitting into" their culture or choosing to look elsewhere. Leading organizations also foster communication more transparently about work-unit-specific results in the areas of safety, quality, patient experience, and engagement, providing performance scores to internal recruiters.

Not every work unit can use this approach to its full advantage, particularly if the team counts more challenges than successes. While leaders of challenged teams might seek to avoid conversations about the obstacles confronting their teams, cultural norms that lead them to speak candidly about current realities redound to their benefit. Many studies[12] have found that providing an unrealistically favorable impression of the work environment is the surest path to regrettable or voluntary turnover. Straightforward managers, by contrast, are more likely to attract successful long-term hires who feel confident that the teams they join will improve over time. In short, high-performing organizations don't simply train their recruiters and leaders in interviewing techniques, but support these leaders by laying out clear expectations and providing information flows, both of which enable transparent conversations with candidates.

In addition, forward-thinking organizations make greater use of prehire assessments, a well-established best practice outside of healthcare. These assessments predict the likelihood that any given applicant will succeed over the long term, reducing selection bias, outperforming human judgments, and bolstering the selection success rate. Historically, healthcare organizations have reserved prehire assessments for management roles, largely out of concern for costs. With new technologies bringing those costs down, and a consensus growing among researchers and patients about the skills and abilities required for future success (Figure 1.1), leading organizations are now assessing candidates for any key roles in which performance disproportionately impacts overall organizational performance.

Emergency department personnel are a good example. Press Ganey has documented that patients admitted to a hospital via the emergency department invariably rate their inpatient experience based, in large part, on their initial interactions with emergency department employees. To ensure a positive first and lasting impression, leading organizations have adjusted their talent management strategy accordingly—a good idea when you consider that high performers are in general *400 percent more productive* than average employees, with the gap widening as job complexity increases.[13] Given that nursing turnover costs organizations roughly $44,000 per nurse, and that nurses directly affect patient quality and safety, leading organizations are now also making fuller use of prehire assessments for those positions as well.

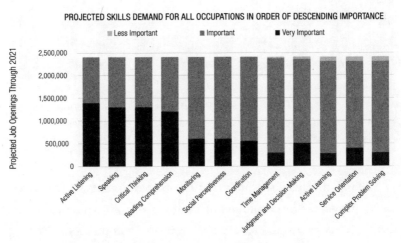

Figure 1.1   Projected Future Skills (adapted from RBC Special Report "Humans Wanted"[14])

Onboard with Purpose

Yet another way that organizations are moving toward strategic talent management is by altering how they onboard employees. Starting a new job is an exciting time for any employee. Press Ganey's national engagement data, comprising more than 1.6 million healthcare workers, indicates that new hires rank as the proudest, most likely to recommend, most satisfied, and most likely to stay with an organization (Figure 1.2). This is hardly surprising. If someone is not excited to start a new job, it's probably the wrong job—or the wrong hire. Our data also reveal that new hires face years of potential disillusionment that only partially rebounds over time; a significant disconnect exists between first impressions and the realities of employment over the course of an employee's first two years. For most employees, perceptions of recognition, fairness of pay, interdepartmental teamwork, involvement, and opportunities for growth quickly erode.[15]

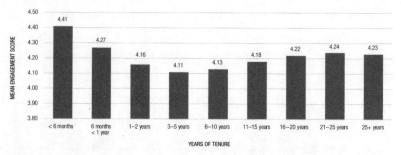

Figure 1.2   Engagement by Tenure of Healthcare Workers (Press Ganey National Data[16])

Many studies also show that the cost of losing an employee in the first year of employment ranges from 20 percent to over 200 percent of annual salary based on job complexity.[17] Recent industry reports reveal that 23.8 percent of all new hires leave after 12 months or prior, representing 32.0 percent of industry turnover, and that just over half (53.3 percent) of workers spend less than two years at their facility.[18] A survey of business leaders showed that only 40 percent of organizations thought their onboarding processes were effective at retaining new talent.[19] The message for talent management is clear: significant opportunities to enhance onboarding exist within the healthcare industry. High-performing organizations have addressed these challenges by creating a wide range of structured experiences to ensure that new hires feel appreciated and are empowered to contribute to organizational performance as quickly as possible.

While many manuals and guides are available to inform the design and improvement of onboarding efforts, certain elements of the onboarding process deserve special mention. Leading organizations ensure that new hires receive far more than the nuts-and-bolts paperwork, policies, and compliance. While paperwork is necessary, best-in-class organizations utilize technology to their advantage to manage the basics so that they can focus on content and relationship building. A robust onboarding program incorporating mission, vision, values, purpose, and the like also affords an opportunity for a variety of roles and professionals to onboard together in a cohort. Talent management leaders should work with their partners in the medical staff offices to ensure that physicians are included as well.

Leading organizations provide ongoing support to new hires by assigning them a mentor and a clinical preceptor during their first year. Mentors foster an understanding of the new employee's role and goals, as well as organizational norms and expectations, while also helping new hires navigate organizational processes and language. Mentors typically help new hires build important relationships within and across departments, ensuring that they become involved in community service projects and similar activities. Managers invest significant time with new hires to ensure that they fit well into their roles, to assess their developmental needs, to gather new-hire insights that might push the department forward, and to provide routine feedback so new hires can conform their work habits to the overall culture. Despite ongoing cost pressures, high-performing organizations "preserve the space" to ensure all employees and physicians are effectively oriented and onboarded to the organization and their department.

Develop and Retain Talent

To render talent management more strategic, leaders should also upgrade how they develop and retain employees. Effective onboarding helps with retention, a significant industry challenge, but it is not enough. One recent study designed to track career changes among new nurses over a 10-year period showed that more than 17 percent of newly minted nurses leave their first post within the first 12 months, 33 percent leave within 24 months, and 60 percent within 8 years.[20] In 2018, the industry witnessed its highest turnover rate in a decade, an average of 18.2 percent for all US hospitals—a level that contrasts sharply with other High Reliability industries like energy (4.9 percent).[21] One national, all-industry study found that the number one reason employees left their jobs in 2017 was a lack of career development opportunities.[22] Such results align well with Press Ganey research that has identified key characteristics of a high-performing culture.[23] Employees and physicians working in these settings feel confident in their job security, enjoy career development opportunities, and believe their organizations provide high-quality care and service.

While current industry outcomes can feel downright disheartening, we can readily overcome them, as we'll see in Chapter 4. A 2019 study found that 94 percent of employees would stay with their employer longer if the company dedicated itself more to their career development (Press Ganey results demonstrate the same).[24] Organizations that capitalize on this interest and enthusiasm through all manner of developmental offerings (like e-, self-paced-, micro-learning job rotation programs; clinical career ladders; action learning projects; and ongoing direct manager-to-employee coaching) are better positioned for success. Similarly, organizations must identify the 10 percent of roles that are pivotal to future organizational success and develop a targeted investment strategy, ensuring that they possess a significant talent pool from which to draw. Finally, as noted previously, career development will remain suboptimal if operational leaders at the highest levels of the organization don't "own" it and take responsibility.

Toward a Resolution

Tidelands Health didn't experience a direct hit when Hurricane Florence made landfall, but the record-setting flooding that ensued required the team to evacuate one of the system's hospitals for a second time just over a week later. "Through it all, our Tidelands Health team showed the dedication, compassion, and grace under pressure that I think would make any leader proud," CEO Bruce Bailey said. "Florence showed us we could deliver when it counted." Patients and employees everywhere likewise count on organizations to deliver when and where it counts. With US unemployment at historic 50-year lows,[25] finding and keeping talented employees remains difficult, and the challenge will only intensify thanks to impending changes in technology, demographics, and care delivery. Unfortunately, too many organizations underestimate the threat, continuing to embrace incremental, transactional, and short-term thinking. Leading healthcare centers have increased investments in their organizational culture and have improved their talent management practices and processes. In the years ahead, they'll have the results to show for it.

IN SUM

- In the coming decades, trends related to technology, demographic change, and care delivery will significantly impact talent management.
- Organizations must adapt their talent management strategies to address these trends or risk being overrun by them.
- Leading organizations strategically manage and adjust their talent management practices, processes, and norms.
- We must address the root causes of employee turnover at each stage of the employee life cycle. This will require numerous and marked changes from current leadership practices.
- High-performing organizations preserve the space and ensure their organizations provide the necessary workforce development for future success.

CHAPTER

2

Engaging People Through Inclusion

Ingrid Summers, MHS

> To improve workforce engagement and attract and
> retain top talent, healthcare organizations must attend to
> issues of diversity, equity, and inclusion throughout the
> talent management life cycle. When organizations pursue
> these efforts thoughtfully, they can harness the powers
> of diverse thinking and collaboration, and advance their
> cultures and missions.

JULIE (NOT HER REAL NAME), an emergency department physician, is a 39-year-old American, born to
an Asian father and Irish mother, both of whom
hail from the Caribbean. A graduate of Morehouse
College's medical school, she's raising a child with her
wife, Janelle, while working a taxing, full-time job.
When Julie first came on board after graduating medical school, she felt excited to join a hospital focused
on bolstering its diversity and inclusion efforts. For its
part, the hospital was happy to hire a candidate who
furthered its goals of increasing the representation of
female physicians and those manifesting other kinds
of diversity.

Two years into Julie's job, hospital leaders invited
her to join a steering committee that addressed

diversity and inclusion within the organization and among medical staff in particular. The organization's chief medical officer (CMO), an older white man and long-term hospital employee, led the committee and its meetings. Although he genuinely sought to improve organizational diversity and inclusion, he tended to dominate conversations, modeling such conduct for other members. The CMO's communication style often led softer-spoken and more reserved committee members to shut down and not contribute to the conversation. The CMO also tended to schedule meetings early in the morning or late in the afternoon, inconveniencing committee members with children.

After a few meetings, Julie began questioning her participation on the committee. Contemplative and an introvert by nature, she needed time to formulate her thoughts, and the conversation often moved on quickly before she could share meaningful feedback. Perceiving her as uninterested in collaborating or unable to do so, her peers began to exclude her from committee decisions and avoid her in social settings, leaving her to think they didn't value her participation or insight. As time passed, Julie grew disillusioned not just with the committee, but with the organization. Her engagement in her job plummeted as she wondered whether her hospital really welcomed people like her. A year or so after joining the committee, she found herself seriously contemplating leaving the organization. "It's sad," she said, "but this hospital isn't what it seemed to be at first. They talk about diversity, but I just don't feel that introverts like me really belong."

As a female person of color, a mother, and a member of the LGBTQ community, Julie is precisely the kind of highly diverse candidate that healthcare organizations actively seek to hire. And yet once they successfully recruit these employees, organizations often fail to engage and retain them. Julie's hospital viewed her ethnicity, parental status, race, sexual orientation, and gender as elements of her diverse profile, but failed to consider the other areas that make her unique. By looking too narrowly at issues of diversity and workplace context, her hospital struggled to create a truly inclusive environment that welcomed Julie in and made her comfortable enough to bring her whole self to work.

This chapter explores the connection between inclusion and caregiver engagement, shedding light on the unconscious bias and microaggressions that often prevent us from creating more inclusive organizational cultures. Our organizations can glean considerable value from diversifying, but diversity alone won't allow them to build engagement. For our increasingly diverse workforces and organizations to thrive, we must also create *inclusive and equitable* work environments. The chapter explores these two concepts and concludes by focusing on how leaders can better welcome and value all employees, leveraging everyone's talents on behalf of patients and the organization.

Understanding Inclusion

Organizations struggle with inclusion in part because many leaders aren't clear about its definition and often conflate it with diversity. Many organizations have attempted to build diverse workforces that mirror the communities they serve, not least because patients prefer to receive care from a physician of the same race.[1] In pursuing diversity, organizations have adopted formal definitions and models for guidance. One popular framework, advanced by Marilyn Loden and Judy Rosener, distinguishes between organizational dimensions of diversity (such as functional level, work location, and seniority), external dimensions (such as parental status, appearance, and educational background), and internal dimensions (such as race, physical ability, and gender). Their framework also includes unique personality traits that organizations should consider when thinking about workforce diversity.[2] Although Loden and Rosener's model is almost three decades old, it remains relevant for healthcare organizations today, as Julie's case suggests. Her race and ethnicity matter, but so do her birth position, family structure, gender identity, educational background, and personality.

Whereas diversity considers many dimensions of a person's identity, inclusion refers to the subjective experience of belonging and feeling valued. As diversity expert Vernā Myers is often quoted as saying, "Diversity is being invited to the party. Inclusion is being asked to dance."[*3] And that invitation is critically important. In a 2017 *Harvard Business Review* article, Laura Sherbin and Ripa Rashid argue that "diversity equals representation" in workplace environments, but in the absence of inclusion, "the crucial connections that attract diverse talent, encourage their participation, foster innovation, and lead to business growth won't happen."[4] If employees receive clear messages that they don't belong, they'll go on the defensive, failing to develop new ideas. They'll feel a nagging sense that their organization and its teams might tolerate them, or like the *idea* of including people like them, but don't really want them. These feelings will diminish their sense of loyalty to the organization and lead them to become less engaged with their work. Organizations must therefore invest time and energy into creating diverse *and* inclusive environments. Diversity alone won't suffice.

With an eye toward inclusion and not simply diversity, we can better appreciate the problem Julie experienced on the steering committee. As a female, LGBTQ-identified physician, she lent much-desired diversity to the committee. But she was overlooked not because of her race, gender, or sexual orientation, but rather her personality or work style. Julie's method of processing information, which included considering all possibilities before providing input, conflicted with the tempo and pace of the CMO's more domineering and brash style. This, in turn, led her colleagues to perceive Julie as failing to add value. As I've noticed throughout my career, managers and colleagues tend to label people like Julie as "introverts," stigmatizing or dismissing them and not inviting them "to dance" in *their* own preferred style. Organizations often talk about creating an environment where people can bring their whole selves to work, but they seldom support people whose "whole self" is different from theirs. It's no wonder people like Julie become disengaged, hampering their organizations' performance.

Think of the tragedy here. Julie's organization invited her to participate in the committee with the best of intentions, but it never allowed her to fully participate. If the CMO had created an inclusive environment by pausing, allotting enough time for everyone to participate, and actively eliciting Julie's feedback, he could have benefited from her thoughtful, well-considered analyses of topics. But that begs the questions: how might he have done this? What does inclusion look like? Before we can answer these questions, we must first bring the concepts of equity and equality into the conversation.

Equity and Equality

Many people conflate these two terms, but they are not the same. Equality is about fairness and justice, ensuring that everyone has access to the same opportunities. To infuse equality into the culture, many organizations have adopted formal statements and implemented policies committing themselves to treating people fairly. The US Office of Personnel Management (OPM), for instance, has adopted the following statement: "[The office] is committed to equal employment opportunity (EEO), in support of OPM's mission to lead and serve the Federal Government in enterprise human resources management by delivering policies and services to achieve a trusted effective civilian workforce."[5] Such statements are a good start, but equality is a limited concept given that not everyone starts from the same place. Some people possess advantages by virtue of their birth or life experience, while others must contend with challenges. Because of this, organizations must not stop at equality, but consider the concept of equity.

Imagine an environment where everyone has access to a five-foot ladder to see over an obstruction—perfect equality—even though they all range between five and six-and-a-half-feet tall. Taller people might not need the ladder, while some of the shorter ones might need an even longer ladder.[6] The concept of equity takes uneven circumstances into account and provides all individuals with the resources they need to succeed. Simply offering employees access to the same resources doesn't mean they'll all be able to make comparable use of them. The concept of equity acknowledges that advantages and barriers exist, and that the organization must strive to correct and address the resultant imbalances. Organizations have tried to treat everyone equally, giving them access to the same resources. It's an improvement over inaction, but far short of equity. Organizations must work to "smooth out" any preexisting advantages and barriers so everyone can truly participate.

National research, for example, shows that LGBTQ patients are at an increased risk of receiving substandard or insensitive care, further exacerbating overall healthcare disparities. To mitigate those disparities and allow for more equitable patient care, Cleveland Clinic began identifying clinicians in their physician directory who were specifically trained in LGBTQ patient-centered care. As Le Joyce Naylor, chief diversity and inclusion officer at Cleveland Clinic, explains, "prior to Cleveland Clinic integrating LGBTQ care into its services, there was no way for an LGBTQ patient to identify a provider who would be sensitive to the unique needs of an LGBTQ individual." By providing equal and equitable care to all patients, Cleveland Clinic's Pride Clinic (LGBTQ), as its best-practice model in LGBTQ care is known, empowers patients with more options, decreasing the chance for disparate care delivery.

Inequities can exist around gender (a group containing many men, but only a few women); role or hierarchy (a mixed group of majority physicians and a few nurses); race (a team with only one person of color); and communications style (groups with a few introverts mingled in with many extroverts). Such inequities confer advantages to members of the majority or dominant group, and disadvantages to members of the minority or subordinate group. In our example, Julie occupied the disadvantaged, or minority group, in an extrovert-dominated space. In my experience, the persistence of inequities prevents disadvantaged people from feeling included in teams and organizations, leading to disengagement. Conversely, data from Cleveland Clinic's engagement surveys show that caregivers who are involved in diversity and inclusion initiatives are more engaged than the general caregiver population.

To promote inclusivity and equity, Julie's CMO might have tried implementing a practice or ground rule like "step up, step up," an approach I have used over the course of my career to encourage full participation from all participants in meetings. Leaders explicitly encourage individuals who dominate a conversation to step up their listening skills, and individuals who are more reserved to step up their contributions. This type of ground rule encourages the expression of all voices and viewpoints.

Organizations should also examine their talent management practices to ensure that they apply an equitable approach to areas like hiring, promotions, and work groups. "Cleveland Clinic aimed to build a leadership team that reflected its caregiver population," says Naylor, "so we took very specific steps to really understand these opportunities." "Our process is to also not just review data by average turnover, promotion, and hire percentages," she adds, "but by race, ethnicity, gender, generational, military, and other demographic categories [as well]." Such an approach ultimately allows the organization to identify the right group of leaders to address the needs of its workforce. As the national and global workforce continues to evolve and diversify, more organizations must design processes and systems that reflect these changes.

Unconscious Bias and Microaggressions

Try as we may to create equitable—and hence inclusive—environments, many organizations still fall short. In part, that's due to two problems: unconscious or implicit bias, and microaggressions. We can define unconscious bias as thoughts or feelings that people automatically hold and apply toward groups of individuals. These thoughts or feelings, whether positive or negative, are outside our conscious control, meaning that offenders aren't actively harboring malice or undeserved praise toward specific groups. Unconscious bias is deeply rooted in our evolutionary history, and necessary for our species' survival. Because our brains process millions of bits of information every moment, we rely on unconscious associations to make automatic decisions steering us away from danger. Unfortunately, our upbringings, media outlets, and other biased sources have caused us to apply these unconscious associations to people of different body sizes, ethnicities, genders, and even organizational positions and roles.

Depending on the situation, unconscious bias can have dire, even catastrophic effects. As illustration, I often cite a *CNN* report about the devastation that Superstorm Sandy wrought in 2012 on Glenda Moore and her family.[7] A nurse and mother, Moore was trapped in a stalled car with her two small children. As the waters continued to rise, she released her children from their car seats and approached nearby houses requesting help. One individual opened the door and then slammed it in her face. Desperate and frantic, Moore ran to the rear door and tried breaking a window, but couldn't. Shortly thereafter, a surge of water ripped her children, ages two and four, out of her arms. They were later found dead nearby. In the *CNN* interview, the homeowner told a reporter that he only saw a man, and that this man threw a concrete flowerpot at his door. The homeowner also told reporters that he had to stay up all night positioned against the door of his house. Glenda Moore was a black woman. The homeowner was not.

While this is an extreme example, people experience unconscious bias every day in healthcare, behaving in ways that negatively impact workforce engagement. It happens every time a man enters a hospital room and is automatically thought to be the physician; every time a woman sits down in the boardroom and is automatically thought to be an assistant; every time an older person is automatically assumed to be too mentally slow to understand a course of treatment; every time someone on a hiring committee declares a "gut feeling" about a (diverse) candidate and decides not to extend an employment offer.

Unconscious bias can compromise the quality and safety of the care we provide to our patients. Consider the case of a 25-year-old woman with a rare congenital disorder and uncontrolled diabetes. Over a year's time, this woman ended up with pancreatitis, which presented with excruciating abdominal pain, leading her to seek treatment in the emergency room. Pancreatitis rarely afflicts a person so young and is typically treated with pain medicine and IV fluids in the ICU. Each time this woman sought care in the emergency room, however, medical staff delayed her treatment and pain medication prescriptions, often considering her a "drug seeker." Unconscious bias likely played a role in these situations. Because of her age, caregivers dismissed pancreatitis and considered her pain as not severe enough to require medication.

As a 2016 Joint Commission newsletter points out, unconscious bias can impact quality of care in many ways: minority patients receive fewer major procedures, like kidney transplants and cardiovascular interventions; black women experience higher mortality rates following the diagnosis of breast cancer;

non-white patients receive fewer pain medication subscriptions; black men receive fewer prostate cancer therapies, like radiation and chemotherapy, and are at increased risk for testicular removal; and minority patients experience more stigmas and prejudice about their supposed "passivity" when it comes to their personal health.[8] In healthcare settings, unconscious bias takes a number of more specific forms, including affinity bias (a natural inclination to be positively disposed to people resembling us); the halo effect (the idea that people we like are fundamentally good people, just because we like them); perception bias (the formation of stereotypes and other preconceptions about certain groups); confirmation bias (our inclination to affirm what we already believe to be true); and groupthink (a tendency to mimic others' opinions or hold back real thoughts and opinions within a particular social setting).

Microaggressions comprise a second barrier to the creation of a diverse, inclusive, and equitable workforce. Merriam-Webster defines a microaggression as "a comment or action that subtly and often unconsciously or unintentionally expresses a prejudiced attitude toward a member of a marginalized group."[9] Despite our best efforts and intentions, we might speak or behave in ways that we don't realize convey our own bias. The following everyday statements contain microaggressions: "What are you?"—when curious about one's race; "Where are you really from?"—when curious about one's ethnicity; "You don't act like a (fill in the blank)"; "Are you old enough to be a doctor?" Such statements might seem innocent, but over time they take an emotional toll, erode morale and engagement, and even give rise to hostile working climates. Although seemingly minor, microaggressions can derail your organization's diversity and inclusion efforts and result in a disengaged workforce.

Julie experienced microaggressions as a medical school graduate of Morehouse College, a historically black college and university. Well-meaning colleagues peppered her with questions like, "What kind of medical school is Morehouse?", "Is it in the United States?", and "What is a historically black college and university (HBCU) exactly?" Although Julie appreciated the interest others took in her background and identity, she came to resent such questions because they suggested that her education and credentials were somehow suspect or less valid. Like many others in her position, she felt she had to constantly educate her colleagues, or worse, defend her choice of school. This is unfair and burdensome, and in her case it contributed to exhaustion and burnout.

Leaning into Inclusivity and Equity

While unconscious bias, microaggressions, and other deep-seated structural inequities might seem difficult or even impossible to rectify, organizations can take several steps to reduce them and to render their organizations more inclusive. Leaders should first make inclusion and equity a strategic priority. Too often, organizations tout the importance of diversity and inclusion initiatives but fail to allocate resources to support them. Creating standalone and capitalized diversity and inclusion strategies aligned with the organization's mission, vision, and values is critical, signaling to all stakeholders that they are priorities. These strategies should also form part of every leader's performance goals, ensuring accountability and follow-through.

Organizations should also clearly define terms, creating common vocabularies and expressions for speaking about diversity, equity, and inclusion in ways that everyone can understand. In addition, organizations should craft formal statements that focus on the importance of both diversity *and* inclusion. Like a vision statement, a diversity and inclusion statement helps provide direction and create a larger ethos. Consider Cleveland Clinic's statement: "Cleveland Clinic values a culture where caregivers integrate diversity and inclusion throughout the enterprise. We respect and appreciate our similarities and differences; they enable us to better serve our patients, one another, and our global communities."[10] Organizations should reinforce such statements by establishing a special council that drives and monitors efforts in these areas. Diversity councils are often composed of members of the diverse groups represented within an organization, advising and serving as the voice of their community. Such councils allow leaders to tap different perspectives and ensure that an organization considers the impact of various initiatives and decisions on its employee and patient populations.

Many organizations have also appointed chief diversity officers, whose job is to focus on diversity and inclusion full-time. This leader should not be embedded in a corporate function, but instead form part of the executive team. The more distanced this individual is from the real decision makers, the harder it is to get the work of inclusion done. By elevating this role to the C-suite, organizations acknowledge the importance of this work. Chief diversity officers aim to set the strategy and vision for diversity, equity, and inclusion efforts and to vocally support teams advancing this work.

Inclusion can feel daunting, so focus your efforts where you find the greatest need. When Dani Monroe, the chief diversity officer at Partners HealthCare, assumed her role six years ago, she began by examining diversity-related representation, termination, and hiring trends, as well as results from employee engagement surveys. She found that perceptions of promotion and development opportunities, primarily at the exempt level and especially among diverse employees, were different from those of their "nondiverse" counterparts. Monroe selected nine questions from the Press Ganey database to include on the organization's next engagement survey to serve as its diversity and inclusion (D&I)

index. With these metrics in place, the organization adopted a strategy for improving diversity and inclusion, focusing on leadership behaviors, an inclusive workforce, and community. Senior leaders developed improvement plans to advance diversity and inclusion within the organization. During her first three and a half years, Monroe socialized the diversity and inclusion initiative, and also educated colleagues and helped enrich their skills. "Leaders need to build an inclusive mind-set and role-model inclusive behaviors," she said. "They need to ensure that they are asking the questions that bring people into the conversation and asking for diverse views."

Organizations should also examine their preexisting practices and policies to ensure that they are bias-free. Further, they should develop a zero-tolerance policy against bullying and ensure that managers conduct job interviews fairly and equitably. In particular, they should leverage interview guides that provide hiring managers with concrete frameworks to compare candidate qualifications, discouraging "a gut feeling" approach. As we know by now, such gut feelings are often linked to unconscious bias. Cleveland Clinic committed several years ago to integrating an awareness of unconscious bias into its talent review and succession planning process. All leaders and managers receive training so that they can mitigate the potential for bias in hiring, promotion, and selection. The organization seeks to create a workforce that welcomes in the communities it serves, and by paying attention to unconscious bias, it has taken an important step.

Reframing the Diversity Narrative

It takes time to make organizations feel more inclusive, just as it does to render them more diverse. Like other cultural efforts, think of these twin priorities as long-term goals. Start the journey by identifying dimensions of inclusivity that deserve special attention, and identifying new practices and policies that might support diversity, equity, and inclusivity. From there, implement the best practices outlined in this chapter. Make diversity and inclusion a priority, hold *all* leaders accountable for diversity and inclusion, and align these objectives with incentives. Educate your workforce on the importance of creating an inclusive environment, develop a common language, adopt a charter/diversity statement, and form a diversity council. It takes effort, and progress might prove uneven. But this is the only way to create working environments where everyone can thrive, giving organizations the full benefit of their energy and engagement.

IN SUM

- Diversity considers many dimensions of a person's identity, while inclusion refers to the subjective experience of belonging and feeling valued.
- Offering employees access to the same resources doesn't mean they'll all be able to make comparable use of them. The concept of equity acknowledges that advantages and barriers exist, and that the organization must strive to correct and address the resultant imbalances.
- To create equitable—and hence inclusive—environments, organizations must address the problems of unconscious or implicit bias and microaggressions.
- Organizations can and should take an array of steps to reduce inequities and render themselves more inclusive.

Defining and Delivering a Comprehensive Engagement Strategy

Shannon Vincent and Lynn Ehrmantraut

> *To improve performance, organizations should adopt a comprehensive strategy that aligns culture and talent with organizational goals. We present five critical steps organizations should embrace when beginning to develop their engagement strategy, as well as when they're reevaluating and bolstering an existing strategy.*

YEARS AGO, WHEN meeting with the chief nursing officer (CNO) of a health system that had recently won the prestigious Malcolm Baldrige award for healthcare quality, a member of our team remarked on the organization's inspiring patient experience results. Why, she asked the CNO, was the organization so successful? "That's easy," the CNO replied. "If it isn't on the strategic plan, it isn't on our radar, and it doesn't get done. So the key for us has been to make patient experience a strategic priority and put it on the plan." To this day, leaders at this organization maintain that the first step to executing any improvement effort well is identifying it as a key strategic priority. Something similar holds true for an organization's efforts to improve engagement and culture in a comprehensive way: if it isn't on the strategic plan, it isn't prioritized and goes unaddressed.

Sadly, many leaders do fail to put their "people strategy" on the strategic plan. They might routinely track metrics, but their goals don't reflect broader efforts to improve the totality of the caregiver experience. Anticipating this reality, we begin our work with client organizations by asking them two questions: "How do you think about and prioritize the development of your people?" and "Why are you conducting an employee survey?" Unclear or unsure responses often follow. The organizations in question often lack any overarching people philosophies, they understand engagement surveys as "check the box" activities, and they don't link delivering a great patient experience with supporting the caregivers responsible for doing so. No surprise that these organizations suffer from high staff turnover, poor team collaboration on care delivery, quality and safety challenges, and subpar financial performance.

Some organizations are different. At Novant Health, a health system headquartered in North Carolina, senior leaders rallied together and decided to act decisively after noticing a dip in engagement scores. They assigned an internal team, prioritized collecting the right data, and developed a comprehensive strategy for partnering with team members to drive engagement. They have linked their people and engagement strategy to the organization's overall goals, adopting the following philosophy: "At Novant Health, people are our business. We treat each other with respect and compassion. We embrace the differences in our strengths while fostering an environment of inclusion, empowerment, inspiration and courage. We always remember, our business is the care of all people, starting with our team members."[1] Tammy Wright, senior director, Voice of the Customer, elaborates, "We need to promote a fully engaged workforce that is inclusive of all, to ensure that we have the right impact on patient experience and fulfill the mission, vision, and values of Novant Health."[2]

Novant's clarity about the importance of this work has led to big improvements in engagement outcomes over a five-year period. The organization has adopted Press Ganey's unified strategy for improving the patient experience, recognizing that engaged, resilient care teams across the continuum enable caregivers to provide patients with safe, high-quality, patient-centered care. Following the steps outlined in this chapter, they have selected the right instruments to survey employees, promoted participation in the survey, and taken action at the system-wide and local levels to improve culture and engagement, including the provision of career path planning programs; human resources (HR) policy revisions that incorporate team member voices; the establishment of resilience training for leaders, providers, and team members; and the creation of yearlong leadership development programs. Employee engagement has soared, moving from the 41st to the 87th percentile. Novant attributes its success to its ability to gather the right information using a comprehensive measurement tool, to take action on the results each and every time, and to continuing to develop leaders to deliver on the overall strategy. Novant's approach, which it calls its "People Credo," drives its entire talent life cycle, ensuring that every leader is "all in, all the time."

Whether you view your workforce as a large line item on an expense sheet or as your organization's greatest asset, you need a comprehensive strategy that aligns culture and talent with organizational goals if you have any hope of improving engagement. Such a strategy is effective because it places the right people in a positive environment and arms them with the right tools. Based on our work with thousands of healthcare organizations across the country, we have identified *five key steps* leaders can take to create a purposeful engagement strategy and improve their organization's ability to deliver safe, high-quality, patient-centered care. Organizations that employ this approach often attain top-quartile engagement performance that leads in turn to top scores in patient experience, safety, and quality. Your organization can achieve similar results as well.

Step 1: Understand Your Current State

Before you can improve engagement, you must first understand how employees at your organization currently feel about their jobs. Leaders should comprehensively audit the organization's past and current approaches to administering, analyzing, reporting, and driving change using employee culture and engagement data and feedback. Leaders should also review historical engagement survey results and identify recent or impending organizational changes that might affect the culture and employee experience, such as executive leadership transitions, large-scale technology implementations, reductions in force, mergers or acquisitions, or changes to compensation packages.

In addition to this information, and before embarking on an improvement journey, leaders must understand whether people-leaders across the organization are ready to effect positive change. We recently worked with a large health system that had suffered through a reduction in force, a wage freeze, multiple departmental restructures, and the departure of several longstanding executives. The pace of change and the lack of a structured and consistent approach to change management led to widespread mistrust and disengagement. As one senior executive commented, "We completely underestimated the impact on our culture. In all the planning discussions, it never came up, but it set us back years from where we could have been in terms of performance."

The traditional, annual, point-in-time action-planning approach stood no chance of rebuilding the culture. So, this organization's leadership team began by creating alignment, developing a cultural learning map that visually represented the organization's identity, purpose, and vision for the future. They developed the learning map over nine months, soliciting input from executives, clinicians, frontline staff, patients, and families. The map thereafter served as the foundation for defining the desired cultural attributes and the skills, competencies, and behaviors necessary to achieve the desired culture. With the map in place, we spent a year working with the organization to codesign and deliver a series of learning and development experiences that created both the skills and the will among employees to adopt the desired "ways of working and interacting" and discard other, less desirable ones. The organization then created multiple channels for sharing information, listening, and responding to frontline employees' concerns, including an internal social networking site, a blog authored by the chief executive officer (CEO), an executive video series, and a purposeful executive rounding program. The process was slow, and it encountered some skepticism and resistance, even among senior leaders. Fortunately, the system's CEO recognized that cultural alignment was not a "nice-to-have," but a strategic imperative. He made the necessary decisions to ensure success.

Four years after this journey began, the organization has not only improved engagement scores but reduced voluntary turnover and improved in nearly every domain of the Hospital Consumer Assessment of Healthcare Providers and Systems (HCAHPS) survey. Achieving all of this, even as the organization continues to experience disruptive change, has convinced the former skeptics. As one such leader remarked, "Having gone through this exercise, I believe we are better positioned for the road ahead. I have never had more confidence in our ability to execute as I do today." Because this particular organization took the time to truly understand the gap between the current and desired states, and then took action to close that gap, it is far better positioned to navigate future disruptive changes in healthcare.

To assess your organization's readiness to shape culture and drive engagement, ask yourself: Are senior leaders prepared to invest their time and energy in this effort *consistently*? Does the broader management team understand the value of improving culture, and can it execute and sustain cultural initiatives successfully? How do leaders typically champion and sponsor change—through talking points, coaching, touch points, or something else? Does the organization make available dedicated resources for managing change, such as a change management professional or a dedicated change management committee? Do managers, teams, and individual employees act on their own to pursue the organization's mission? Has the organization implemented large-scale change in the past, and how might those previous experiences impact current initiatives? Posing such questions should help the organization identify and address potential barriers to driving engagement and shaping the desired organizational culture.

Step 2: Put in Place the Appropriate Measurement Tools and Methodologies

Reflecting on the overall strategy, leaders must deploy a comprehensive measurement regimen, including an initial deep-dive diagnostic and follow-up pulse surveys. As Pamela Hardy, Novant Health's vice president of Learning and Development, noted, her organization sought to forge a strong connection between "talent management, engagement, and patient experience strategies."[3] Measurement supported her organization's overall "trifecta" of consumers, patients, and providers, helping the organization attract and retain the right talent to fulfill its missions. Novant Health now employs a holistic approach in its strategic initiatives, with its measures revealing connections among diverse areas like engagement, work environment, safety, and resilience. The resultant managerial interventions are much more precise than the "shotgun" measures leaders had formerly implemented.

As we'll explore further in Chapter 5, strong measurement tools are firmly grounded in science, and they track current performance in the context of factors or "key drivers" that most impact employees' work environments, such as whether employees trust their leadership, strive for excellence at work, and have input into major decisions affecting job roles. Unvalidated, pop-up technology companies often invite you to "write your own survey," but their products can lead to unwise investments and unhelpful, do-it-yourself projects. A quick pulse survey that poses a handful of questions to a targeted group of employees on an ad hoc topic can help leaders assess a team's perspective on a particular issue or determine whether previous interventions have yielded results. While forming part of a comprehensive measurement strategy, these pulse surveys can't replace the robust measurement that high-performing organizations use, which includes reliable and validated instruments. Solid measurement surveys provide an overall, outcome-based engagement metric as well as the ability to segment results to identify bright spots and growth areas among work units and work-unit leaders. These surveys also measure top organizational priorities, realities impacting the workforce, and impressions among unique clinical staff segments, such as nurses and physicians.

Leaders should employ open-ended survey questions to encourage qualitative comments from employees about strengths and improvement opportunities. These comments can provide rich examples and stories illustrating employee needs, potentially driving communication throughout the employee life cycle as outlined later in this chapter. Ensure that your survey's demographic data enable segmentation by types of individuals in order to understand variation in key metrics. Consider demographic variables that might prove illuminating, such as length of service, age groups, gender, or work shift. Including nontraditional demographic filters can also help you test interventions. You could, for example, segment the data by employees who attended a wellness retreat, enrolled in a new onboarding program, or participated in a leadership course, or you could align culture and engagement data to other metrics like manager performance ratings to get a more informed and holistic view of performance. Such analyses will generate a rich body of knowledge and a valuable return on investment.

The amount and frequency of data collection hinge on your organization's capability and willingness to act upon data-driven insights. Leaders who combine measurement with action win trust among employees, while those who measure but fail to act, don't. High-performing organizations focused on driving maximum value usually conduct a full census survey every year, adding at least one pulse survey to gauge the impact of these actions. *Impact pulse* surveys occur halfway between full census surveys and measure the efficacy of improvement planning (for instance, "This organization has made positive changes as a result of the feedback from the culture and engagement survey"), as well as topics important to organizational improvement planning. *Life-cycle pulse* surveys assess key events in the employee life cycle. They might gauge how new hires feel about onboarding and enculturation, or why departing employees decided to leave (similar, in this case, to a typical "exit interview"). Organizations should also conduct ad hoc *micro-pulse* surveys to solicit employee insight for a specific purpose, like an upcoming town hall meeting or current initiative. High-performing organizations act on and communicate survey results, no matter whether a survey is full census or micro-pulse. When they don't act, caregivers can tire of sharing their opinions, perceiving that doing so will make little difference—a phenomenon we call "inaction fatigue."

Step 3: Establish a Deliberate, Comprehensive, Consistent Communication Plan

In addition to having a strong measurement system in place, leaders should plan how they will communicate about engagement to the organization. All employees must understand why they're participating in a culture and engagement survey; how the related improvement efforts will support broader organizational imperatives around safety, quality, and experience of care; what their roles are; and how they will benefit. When organizations don't highlight the rationale for an engagement survey, and when leaders don't demonstrate their commitment, the effort often loses momentum, becoming "just another survey." Successful organizations leverage a strong communication plan throughout the process, from the initial announcement, to the rollout of the results, to the improvement plan's execution.

One exemplary organization we partnered with aligned the look and feel of their survey communications with their employer branding materials. Leaders there treated engagement data as a key source of insight into the employee experience and the branding strategy's effectiveness. The executive team communicated with frontline staff via videos, emails, and rounding, delivering face-to-face talking points to frontline staff during the last of these. Their messages were clearly aligned, on brand, and updated throughout the year. Thanks to these efforts, this organization consistently scores in the top quartile for engagement and improvement planning effectiveness.

Less successful organizations skip communication planning entirely and scramble to communicate at the last minute, leaving the impression of a disconnected, improvised effort. One organization asked us to conduct post-survey focus groups with staff members to better understand the story behind the data. Over multiple sessions, it became clear that employees were seeing engagement scores for the first time. Several employees also had no clue why leaders had asked them to participate in the focus group. This disconnect between intent and execution reflected a lack of communication planning. Developing your communication strategy well in advance and allocating resources will enable your organization to focus on the narrative rather than the mechanics once engagement data are released.

Communications matter throughout the measurement process. Prior to the survey, leaders should build awareness and support by providing employees with a sense of the survey's relevance and broader context. When administering the survey, focus employees on the survey's value and the confidentiality of their responses, using talking points, survey ambassadors, visual reminders, senior leader rounds, and incentives for participation. Managers can deploy talking points during huddles, in emails, and on rounds to keep teams informed and excited about the survey process. Following the conclusion of the survey, the CEO and executive team should circulate a notice to all staff, thanking them for taking the time to share and provide feedback, and previewing next steps, such as when the results will be shared, what they plan to do with the results, and what follow-up activities employees can expect.

As we'll see in Chapter 6, high-performing organizations publicize the data progressively, telling a compelling story along the way that connects cultural improvement efforts with other key initiatives and work streams. One of our client organizations started with a targeted, executive-level communication to tell the "story behind the data," connecting the results to safety and patient experience trends and identifying key areas for improvement. In its initial results communication, the executive team highlighted past efforts to improve safety, based on previous results, explaining how those efforts helped improve employee engagement and reduce risk to patients and caregivers. With that framing in place, leaders then revealed that they had recently uncovered that some in the workforce lacked trust in leadership and were determined to address it. In a series of town halls, leaders guided discussions around these topics, teasing out both the root causes and proposed solutions. One town hall attendee shared feedback stating, "Thank you for giving us this time. For the first time in my career, I can say I believe my leaders really care what I have to say. It feels good to know my words will actually make a difference."

Leaders at high-performing organizations continue to communicate with employees on an ongoing basis, providing progress updates and recognizing exemplary leaders and departments for their improvement efforts. As these leaders partner with their teams to execute on their improvement plans, they continue to connect execution with safety, clinical excellence, and the patient experience. By creating a single, all-encompassing narrative, leaders can rally frontline employees around a single message, winning hearts and minds and channeling the workforce's creative energies.

Step 4: Leverage Data to Inform and Align Talent Strategies

In Chapter 1, we discussed how strategic talent management helps advance an organization's culture. Many steps in the talent management cycle—recruiting, hiring, onboarding, development, recognition/rewards, and succession management—offer opportunities in this regard, allowing leaders to maximize returns on investment. Leaders should match metrics at the work-unit level with turnover rates to identify underlying themes and reasons for attrition and retention. They should use data to identify leaders who need additional development and coaching, and to guide ongoing strategy development for specific groups or talent life-cycle processes. Finally, they should act to capitalize on data-driven trends, adjusting new-hire programming, retention efforts, or investments in leader development. Let's examine these key talent management steps in turn.

First, leaders should use current HR metrics, including culture and engagement survey results, to identify gaps in attracting talent. They should focus attention on high-value services or roles targeted for growth, or services or roles that are hard to fill, developing strategic recruiting plans to bridge any gaps. To supplement insights gathered from the data, HR leaders should ask themselves several questions, including: How does the labor market currently regard the organization? How does the organization compare to competitors? Is the organization creating a narrative aligned with its mission, identity, and patient promise? Is the organization's talent pool lacking in certain demographic groups, and is that lack of diversity limiting performance?

When selecting new hires, leaders can also mobilize data advantageously. Hiring managers should ask, "What messages are candidates receiving (perhaps unintentionally) about how they are viewed, and about what it might be like to work at the organization?" When interviewing, consider sharing data from the culture and engagement survey to convey the strengths of the work-unit environment, how teams address challenges, and any progress updates. By painting a realistic but positive picture of the organization, you can reduce attrition later on. Results from candidates and hiring manager surveys can also uncover ways to optimize the hiring process, improving communications and decision-making. Data from highly engaged work units can illuminate the employee attributes and leadership competencies that lead to employee success, allowing you to select for such traits during the hiring process and (when used alongside talent assessments and performance evaluations) improve your development programming curricula. Consider surveying your new hires to identify any unwelcoming, uninspiring, or uninformative messaging they encountered. Ask unsuccessful job applicants to fill out these surveys, as they will likely have valuable insights into your process. Surveying them might also allow you to stay connected and possibly hire them for other roles, bolstering your employer brand in the process.

During and after the onboarding phase, high-performance organizations solicit feedback from employees, asking them about the content, pacing, flow, and delivery of information about the organization. Follow up by assessing the enculturation process as it unfolds, fielding new-hire (life-cycle) pulse surveys at 30, 60, and 90 days after an employee's hire, and asking about each employee's level of engagement, social support, knowledge gaps, and current needs. After onboarding, when employees are forming beliefs about the organization and its culture, seek feedback about their experiences so they feel supported and so you can help retain them. Emphasize the organization's investment in retention, engagement, safety, quality, and patient experience. Doing so during one-on-one employee meetings or during team events can build loyalty among employees, increase positive word of mouth, and boost performance. Our patient experience data, for example, show that stronger teams generate better patient experiences.

If new hires manage work units or departments in the organization, HR/organizational development leaders should review work-unit survey results as part of the onboarding experience. This will help recently hired managers understand their reports' expectations and needs and identify areas to probe during team meetings. Reviewing work-unit survey results with newly hired managers also helps reinforce the expectation that improving culture and engagement is critical for success in their new roles. Upon reviewing annual or pulse engagement results, and throughout the year, work-unit leaders should discuss findings with their teams, probe for additional insights, and engage the team in meaningful improvements that will further drive engagement.

Organizations can also leverage engagement data to develop and retain employees. During a recent employee engagement survey at Novant Health, talent leaders found that although most nurses were quite engaged, certified nurse assistants (CNAs) felt they had limited personal and professional development opportunities and didn't know about the resources available to them. The organization responded by developing a CNA-to-RN career-progression program, improving engagement and sense of belonging among these nurses, while also increasing the RN pool available to the organization. To discover needed career development resources that your organization might not offer, consider polling employees about the resources they'd appreciate. Organizations should also monitor internal and external information sources, including engagement surveys, exit interviews, trends in turnover rates, and comments on external sites such as Glassdoor and Indeed.

Step 5: Track Integrated Metrics and Quantify Return on Investment (ROI)

Many organizations fixate on engagement scores as the sole measures of the survey's effectiveness and that of the improvement planning process. As we'll discover in Chapter 5, while the engagement score is a valuable metric to include on board scorecards and key performance indicator sheets, focusing excessively on it and "chasing a score" might frustrate leaders and staff and stall progress. Organizations should quantify progress and measure the success of their engagement strategies in more varied and targeted ways. When thinking about ROI, revisit your initial goals and then develop a micro-scorecard that includes clear criteria reflecting those goals. The organization's initial objectives should influence how it tracks progress and measures the success of its overall engagement strategy.

If your initial goal is to develop leadership competency, for instance, create a management behaviors scorecard that includes criteria that impact employee engagement, such as inclusion, respect, trust, coaching, and recognition. Quantify investments in leadership, such as training time and materials and executive coaching, and track improvements in employees' ratings of their managers on selected competencies. Measure and assess, when possible, the financial impacts of staff-related investments, such as improved frontline retention rates and decreased costs related to recruiting/training new talent. These metrics should improve with the additional investment in professional development.

If your organization seeks to improve patient experience and loyalty, assess metrics related to those goals, identifying units where changes are taking hold and those where additional work is necessary. By incorporating vital culture, engagement, and patient experience metrics into a single framework, leaders can compare work-unit performance, identify inconsistencies across metrics, and track progress over time.

If your organization seeks to build a culture of safety, a scorecard might include cultural components like trust, psychological safety, accountability, and a learning culture. Improvement planning on these topics should impact engagement but also lead to greater frequency of error reporting, more frequent accountability behaviors that prevent errors, and fewer serious safety events. Measure realized reductions in safety events against improvements on critical elements of safety culture.

If your organization seeks to positively influence workforce metrics and their related financial indicators, conduct an impact analysis. A facility-level analysis can tie culture and engagement metrics directly to financial performance metrics such as operating margin and revenue growth. Translate common workforce metrics into financial terms to assess their impact (for instance, cost of absenteeism per employee turnover/average cost of hire).

To monitor progress over time, consider implementing interim measures such as pulse surveys, quarterly reviews, follow-up focus groups, and other data sources. Commit to a regular cadence in which you review the scorecard and assess progress toward goals.

Conclusion

It really is true: if you want people in your organization to take something seriously, you must put it on the strategic plan. This chapter's framework will help ensure that everyone in your organization considers caregivers and their experience, so that your workplace culture can improve in turn. Leaders at high-performing organizations like Novant Health recognize that proceeding strategically and prioritizing people produces better outcomes in safety, quality, and patient experience. Advancing culture and engagement using the steps we've outlined, your organization can accelerate and sustain its improvement efforts, integrating real-time improvement strategies into leaders' daily routines, and making a concern for workplace culture part of *everyone's* job.

IN SUM

- A strategic approach begins with understanding the current culture and identifying how it deviates from the desired culture.
- Based upon this analysis, the organization should purposefully and strategically select the appropriate measurement tools and methodologies.
- Leaders must craft a deliberate and comprehensive communication plan to ensure that everyone understands the purpose of the measurement, the improvement work to follow, and progress the organization is making toward its goals.
- Use engagement data to quantify the impact of investments and to inform key parts of your talent strategy. Top-performing organizations use integrated scorecards with diverse metrics derived from their original goals.

Strengthening Transformational Leadership

CHAPTER

4

Eric W. Heckerson, EdD, RN, FACHE,
and Brad Pollins, MS, SPHR

> Traditional, "transactional" leadership can no longer
> meet the needs of today's caregivers and patients. We
> need transformational approaches instead. To improve
> engagement, leaders must become nimbler as well as
> more culturally focused, strategic, employee- and patient-
> centric, and proactive in meeting stakeholder needs.

BECKY, A SEASONED nurse leader, never forgot the
day she expressed concern about a patient's care. A
78-year-old man had presented in the emergency
room struggling to breathe, with an extremely rapid,
irregular heart rate; a wet cough; and fluid in his legs
and abdomen. The care team—including a cardiologist, hospitalist, and nurse—stabilized him and then
huddled outside the patient's room discussing treatment options. Their conversation grew heated as the
cardiologist and hospitalist vehemently disagreed on
the best course of treatment. Evidently, the patient
and his wife overheard the exchange, because when
Becky glanced into the patient's room, she noticed a
tear streaming down his cheek and fear on his wife's
face. She entered the room to comfort them both.
"Don't worry," she said, "I'll be your eyes and ears.

We'll make sure that you receive the best care possible and I will keep you safe."

When Becky later described this experience at a department committee meeting, her colleagues in the room fell silent—they knew the organization had not delivered the kind of experience this patient and his family deserved. The committee decided then and there to commit formally to treating patients and one another politely, compassionately, and professionally. They developed a compact that included specific behaviors such as discussing the patient's treatment plan privately, agreeing on the treatment plan before discussing the course of action with the patient, warmly greeting the patient and family members, sitting down to talk to the patient, using a gentle touch and reassuring words during these conversations, and expressing confidence in other team members' skills and abilities.

The committee felt excited about this compact, but when they shared it with others on the unit, the response was underwhelming. Team members greeted the compact cynically, assuming that the committee wasn't serious and that this imperative was "just words." Team members agreed to comply, and at first, they made good on their commitment in a superficial way. They smiled in front of patients and demonstrated a few of the behaviors, but their actions didn't seem authentic. Over a few months' time, this changed. The number of positive team interactions increased, and smiles now seemed genuine. The number and quality of positive comments about patient experience also increased. The overwhelming theme in these comments became "the staff treat you with compassion; it's like you're a member of their family."

Reflecting on this episode, Becky realized that her leadership style needed to change. She had to spend more time with her people, embedding her organization's desired, patient-centric culture by role modeling, observing, coaching, and encouraging.

She decided to follow the widely accepted 80/20 rule, spending 80 percent of her time with team members and 20 percent of her time on administrative tasks. Leaders, Becky realized, needed to be purposeful, deliberate, and disciplined if they were to drive both successful outcomes and broader, transformational change.

Most healthcare leaders take a traditional, transactional approach to leadership, focusing on tactics and day-to-day operations while using rewards and punishments to encourage desired behaviors. Such leadership approaches typically don't foster high levels of engagement and performance, and they also fail to motivate or inspire team members to embrace dramatic cultural change. So-called transformational leaders, by contrast, obtain far better results by communicating compelling visions about the future, modeling the behaviors needed to reinforce the desired organizational culture, motivating team members through intensive one-on-one coaching, and encouraging employees to become active thinkers and contributors.

As effective as these transformational leaders are, most organizations have trouble developing them. With patient expectations, evidence-based practices, demographics, competition, technologies, and demand for services constantly in flux, and with the structures and regulations of medical professions adding further complexity, most leaders today struggle to stay afloat, let alone focus on larger missions and organizational visions. Despite these challenges, this chapter invites you to imagine a healthcare industry in which everyone works in sync with the organizational purpose, and in which transformational leaders navigate challenges, uncover exciting new possibilities, engage workforces, and transform the cultures of their organizations. To help make this dream a reality, we'll describe the essential characteristics of a transformational leader and offer practical advice leaders can adopt to evaluate their current level of effectiveness and identify growth opportunities.

Transactional Versus Transformational Leadership

Let's first distinguish between transactional and transformational leadership a bit more closely. Julie, a seasoned, experienced, and capable charge nurse in a busy urban emergency department, is what we might call a transactional leader. She spends her 12-hour shift "putting out fires," fixing problems, and directing patient traffic. Essentially, she supports the *status quo*, maintaining the normal flow of operations and managing employee behavior through punishments and rewards. Embroiled in the minutiae of the day and mired in operational details, she's too "busy" to think much about the organization's broader strategy, including the safety and patient-centered initiatives that she is supposed to help implement during her shifts. As a result, she leaves it to her department manager to worry about the "bigger picture." While leaders like Julie can thrive in the fray, they usually fail to build relationships with staff, bolster overall engagement, and build cultures that inspire employees to put in their best work.

We would hardly suggest that all transactional leadership practices are outdated or inappropriate. Many of these practices, such as a focus on goals, a problem-solving orientation, and an emphasis on compliance with rules, do help teams operate efficiently and achieve performance targets. But because transactional leaders lack a broader perspective of their role and a deeper understanding of how to foster a people-centered culture, they can't drive the changes organizations need to perform at their best. Our patients and all of our team members deserve farsighted leaders who understand the "bigger picture," are determined to drive cultural improvement, and recognize that great behaviors produce great outcomes. We deserve leaders who intentionally orchestrate a culture that elicits the very best from the workforce, and who do so not by dictating it, but by collaborating with, building trust with, and inspiring employees and leaders at every level. We deserve what we and other management thinkers have termed transformational leaders, as distinguished in Table 4.1.

Table 4.1   Differences Between Transactional and Transformational Leadership

Transactional	Transformational
Goal-focused (what)	Purpose-focused (why)
Focused on challenges	Focused on possibilities
Disseminates information	Engages in conversation
Builds relationships	Makes genuine connections
Builds compliance through rules	Builds commitment through trust
Sees limitations (enhances weaknesses)	Sees potential (enhances strengths)
Intellectual stimulation	Emotional stimulation

Carla, a medical-surgical director, engages her staff in creating the unit's purpose and vision because she understands that people support what they help create. She pays particular attention to purpose, ensuring that everyone knows the "why" of what they are doing, so that they will feel motivated to collaborate in achieving something special. In fact, Carla expects her staff to do three things exceptionally well: live the purpose, embody the values, and discharge the job in a patient-centric way. She continually engages her staff to think about the values and practice the behaviors needed to create an excellent patient experience. Unlike the typical transactional leader, Carla spends most of her time on the unit observing staff behaviors and interactions. She accentuates the positive through appreciative inquiry and invites staff to reflect on what they did well and how they might grow more and achieve even higher degrees of excellence. Always prioritizing team culture, Carla rigorously selects and diligently retains employees who fit the team's cultural standards.

Three Themes of Transformational Leadership

Although the specific behaviors transformational leaders embrace are many and varied, we can distinguish three essential aspects of transformational leadership: leading *self*, leading *people*, and leading *transformation*. This simple template can assist hiring managers during the interview process, throughout the training and development phase, and in the annual review process when evaluating a leader's effectiveness. Successful and effective leaders first develop the capacity to lead themselves. Only then can they develop the skill and aptitude for leading others, going on to advance new processes, operations, and organizational strategies ("leading transformation"). This section discusses a set of competencies that revolve around these three categories, outlined in Table 4.2.

Table 4.2   Three Aspects of Transformational Leadership

Category	Leadership Competency
Leading **Self**	1. Applying emotional intelligence to your role 2. Maintaining and enriching resilience 3. Ensuring ethics and personal integrity
Leading **People**	4. Leading strategically and managing others 5. Communicating effectively 6. Managing conflict 7. Building a high-performing and diverse team 8. Coaching others and giving (and receiving) feedback
Leading **Transformation**	9. Solving problems, thinking critically, and making data-based decisions 10. Managing change and fostering innovation 11. Improving process, safety, flow, and operations

Leading Self

Although countless books, courses, and certifications help organizations develop leaders, leaders do best when they design their own, customized leadership development plans. Leading self, as we conceive it, involves the cultivation of self-knowledge—an awareness of one's own strengths, opportunities, interests, aspirations, and goals—followed by the individual's exploration of what makes for a successful and effective leader, and the crafting of a customized plan that individuals can use to learn, develop, and discover. To begin with, leaders should study and master the art and science of emotional intelligence. Since Pater Salovey and Jack Mayer introduced the concept in 1990, emotional intelligence has played a prominent role in developing highly effective, communication-centered leaders. Daniel Goleman, who popularized the concept, joins Richard Boyatzis and Annie McKee in characterizing emotional intelligence as "how leaders handle themselves and their relationships."[1] Goleman and others argue that people with higher levels of emotional intelligence (often abbreviated as EQ) tend to be more successful, productive, and well-grounded than their counterparts. Table 4.3 provides a high-level summary of actions that leaders can take to enhance their EQ.

Table 4.3   Specific Actions for Increasing Emotional Intelligence (EQ)

Element of Emotional Intelligence	Simplified Explanation	Actions to Take
Self-Awareness	Know Yourself and Your Emotions	1. Take an honest look at yourself. 2. Know your strengths and weaknesses. 3. "Look in the mirror." 4. Work on any deficits.
Self-Management	Know How to "Control" Yourself	5. Don't get too angry or jealous. 6. Know what pushes your buttons. 7. Avoid impulsive decisions. 8. Be thoughtful. Be comfortable with change.
Motivation	Are Motivated by Long-Term Wins	9. Choose long-term success over short-term success. 10. Be productive and seek challenges.
Empathy	Understand Others	11. Recognize feelings in others. 12. Master the art of listening. 13. Avoid stereotyping or judging.
Social Skills	Know How to Communicate with Others	14. Develop others. Help them shine. 15. Develop communication skills. 16. Build relationships (wide and deep).

We often can't control the events that transpire during our leadership tenure, as well as their consequences. We *can* control how well we know ourselves, how well we know others, and how well we manage our relationships as we respond to unpredictable circumstances. When an event happens, pause and ask yourself: What outcome do I want? Based on the answer, choose the actions that will maximize your likelihood of achieving your desired outcome. Mobilizing EQ, you can dramatically enhance your own effectiveness and model for others how best to respond to events.

In addition to developing EQ, you must also cultivate a better understanding of your own goals and values to properly lead yourself. Consider crafting a personal values statement outlining three or four themes to guide your personal leadership journey. Such a statement might begin as follows: "I commit to carrying out my role as leader with integrity, honesty, fairness, and passion." Rehearse this statement often to remind yourself of your personal leadership style. Frame it and keep it on your desk or attach it to your bulletin board. Identifying and recording your values helps cement a strong and enduring leadership philosophy.

You should also think carefully about ethical standards of behavior, and apply them consistently to your own actions. Integrity is a foundational attribute of any high-performing and transformational leader. Which ethical qualities do you especially value? What is your own personal code of conduct? As a leader you will probably come across many situations that can pose a challenge to your integrity. Remember to always be honest in your dealings with others. Do what you say, act in the best interest of your patients, and always do the right thing (even when nobody is watching). You will be laying the foundation for transformational leadership, building a capacity to inspire and motivate others to make positive change.

Leading People

While personal leadership undergirds highly effective leadership in general, leading others is the "heart" of a transformational leader's work. Leaders are typically charged with carrying out a mission to advance an agenda and ensure the organization's success. But there is often latitude in "how" a leader will lead and what leadership style and philosophy will ultimately prevail. To become a transformational leader, formulate your own working definition of leadership. Definitions of leadership vary, but they often include common leadership traits like honesty, energy, optimism, creativity, inclusivity, compassion, and a passion for results. At leadership development workshops, we've asked attendees to list traits that characterized the "best leader" they have encountered in their careers. Their lists have typically included many of the traits listed previously, along with hands-on energy, good communication skills, and a collaborative spirit. Asked to identify traits of the "worst leader" they have encountered, attendees usually list traits such as lack of integrity, passion, energy, and so forth.

To become adept at leading others, transformational leaders must understand in particular how to supervise others in ways that inspire optimal performance. A high-performing team with a transformational leader at the helm states a clear mission, includes the right people, ensures buy-in from everyone, recognizes good work, operates in a safe environment, and often challenges the status quo. When supervising others, a transformational leader ensures that direct reports understand exactly what is expected of them. They make no secret of how they define individual success, and they ensure that individuals know their role in and importance to the greater team mission. Such leaders facilitate candid conversations about expectations from the very beginning, ensuring buy-in and commitment from the outset.

In general, communicating well is crucial for maintaining individual accountability. If an employee has committed to do something, act in a certain way, or adhere to a particular set of policies, and they don't deliver, you can provide feedback. A leader might ask, "When you were hired, you agreed to these clear expectations, but lately you have not been fulfilling them. How can I help you recommit?" Be specific in addressing any deficits, and collaborate with employees to ensure they can succeed. Some organizations use the term *nonnegotiables* to identify required behaviors that employees simply must adopt. Leading transformation and building a culture around trust and accountability requires such clarity along with ongoing, direct feedback and coaching. As we've found, this cycle of expectations and accountability is critical for driving and sustaining performance.

Transformational leaders must also manage conflict, addressing disruptive behaviors and helping their employees exemplify the attributes of a transformational leader. This process starts with leaders role-modeling important leadership traits and behaviors, as well as controlling their own anger and jealousy. Leaders must understand what triggers them emotionally and understand how to intercede in the moment. Habits that help include taking "mindful moments" during which leaders breathe deeply and even recite a personal mantra to calm and recenter themselves. Transformational leaders can make measured and thoughtful decisions even when triggered, resolving conflict in ways that serve the group's best interests.

Transformational leaders also become adept at building high-performing teams that align with an organization's True North. In particular, transformational leaders embrace a number of behaviors that yield high performance, including setting a clear mission, engaging the right players, ensuring buy-in from everyone, overcommunicating, and using data and measurement tools during decision-making. Leaders of high-performing teams focus on selecting team members of different backgrounds and experience who bring diverse perspectives to problem-solving and care delivery. Leaders allow these team members the autonomy they need to accomplish the daily standard work within their job functions. Transformational leaders also focus on team building and allow for equitable input on decisions that affect the team.

A final way transformational leaders lead people more effectively than transactional leaders is by delivering coaching and feedback. Recall that Becky, the nurse leader, began spending more time with her staff, observing, evaluating, and coaching team members for greater effectiveness. During our work with clients, we spend a great deal of time helping leaders develop these skills on their journey to becoming more transformational. Partnering with a coach from Press Ganey, John Muir Health began a formal coaching and development program in 2015. Following a series of cohort-based and one-on-one coaching sessions, 53 leaders showed significant improvement in their overall engagement indicator scores, their "leader scores," and their "team index" outcomes. The participating leaders' work elevated their collective engagement mean score from 3.60 to 4.16 in just a few months.

Providing feedback is one of the most important leadership tasks, enabling improvement and bolstering engagement. Every individual deserves progress updates, corrections of suboptimal behavior, and praise for a job well done. Some experts suggest that leaders provide three pieces of positive praise for every piece of constructive feedback. At Press Ganey, we promote a 5:1 ratio as a High Reliability leadership tactic. Leadership coach Kim Scott, author of the book *Radical Candor*, argues that providing direct and blunt feedback ensures that messages are relayed without extraneous noise or intention.[2] In an effort to be nice, we sometimes avoid having conversations that individuals need and deserve. We advise a number of best practices, including making feedback a ubiquitous part of the culture, planning your remarks without overthinking them, providing feedback in the moment, and delivering it from a place of caring and higher purpose.

Leading Transformation

The third and final aspect of transformational leadership, leading transformation, encompasses business, functional, and enterprise-level roles. The specific duties related to transformation vary according to leaders' status and position within the organization, but our experience shows that leaders must possess strong problem-solving and critical-thinking skills to lead transformations, and that they must be adept at making data-based decisions. Managing change, fostering innovation, and addressing the process and operational needs of the team are also vital to effecting transformation.

Transformational leaders approach problems differently than other leaders do. They evaluate situations and make decisions with a keen eye toward advancing the organization's purpose, culture, and strategies, asking critically minded questions like: "What do I not understand that I need to understand about this problem?", "What do others understand about the problem that will help me see it differently?", and "What do I see that I am denying because I am committed to a certain paradigm?" Transformational leaders also consider problems from all angles, scanning the environment, considering all stakeholders, and marshaling relevant data. Transactional leaders might apply *some* of these lenses in the course of their daily work, but by no means all. Transformational leadership requires that leaders think broadly and deeply, bringing as much knowledge as possible to bear when making decisions.

As generally skilled as they are, transformational leaders are especially sophisticated when it comes to managing change and fostering innovation. Most leaders flounder here, in large part because they fail to communicate change efforts well. In our work with leaders, we deploy a framework called the 5 Ps to improve communication in times of significant change. Leaders should convey the *purpose* (What is the purpose of the change effort? Why are we doing this and why now?); the *picture* (What is the primary goal we are trying to accomplish?); the *plan* (What approach will help us best achieve the vision?); the *prize/penalty* (What is the upside of success and the downside of failure?); and the *part to play* (What is required of each stakeholder or stakeholder group?).

In the following sample communication, note how the leader has used the 5 Ps to bolster physician engagement, a critical driver of safe, high-quality, patient-centered outcomes:

> Team, our purpose is to help physicians feel valued and unencumbered. We believe this will increase their ability to deliver a great patient experience (purpose). Our vision is to elevate physician engagement from the 50th to the 75th percentile by the end of the year (picture). Our plan to achieve this goal is to (1) identify what physicians value most, (2) uncover frustrations, and (3) deploy solutions addressing 1 and 2 (plan). If successful, our team will serve as internal benchmarks of excellence in safety, quality, and patient experience. If we fail, we'll continue performing at our current level or experience performance decreases (prize/penalty). We need you to become an active participant in the process because we value your opinion, ideas, and wisdom and you can help positively encourage others in this effort (part to play).

By using such a framework, leaders clarify the why, what, and how of transformation for all to digest. Modify this messaging formula to serve different audiences and stakeholders in your organization. Use one-on-one influencing conversations as well, emphasizing a person's role or function in the organization and how they can benefit from contributing to organizational change. Enhancing and streamlining communication helps drive change and engagement, paramount objectives for transformational leaders.

Using the 5 Ps, leaders can guard against sending mixed signals. A signal refers to a behavioral or practice-based cue that conveys something's importance and influences others' thoughts and behaviors. Leaders should know that they constantly emit signals, and that certain signals can undermine the organization's transformation efforts and larger cultural goals. We can distinguish here between "pull" and "push" signals. A pull signal allures others to take part in a movement, while push signals constitute directives to comply with larger changes. Throughout your organization, contradictory signaling likely abounds. When stated values and leadership behaviors differ, team members tend to take their cues from how leaders behave. What leaders tolerate also strongly affects organizational culture. Remember: what is permitted, persists. Great leaders align their behavior to support a robust culture, energizing others to do the same.

A final way that transformational leaders push forward change efforts is by improving processes and addressing operational inefficiencies. Transformational leaders acknowledge that broken or poorly designed processes prevent organizations from performing at their best. They work collaboratively with employees to identify and remove obstacles, constraints, and barriers that drain energy, create workarounds, and cause employees and patients high levels of frustration.

When it comes to efficiency, transformational leaders choose to focus on a "vital few" priorities as opposed to pursuing sporadic goals simultaneously. The latter leads to initiative overload, and in turn, drains energy and focus. Leaders must prioritize what matters, cascading responsibilities to ensure that everyone understands their precise role. Leaders should also ensure that accountability standards explicitly express how employees can contribute to the organization's and department's "vital few." Leaders should engage employees in frequent one-on-one performance discussions and devote a significant portion of the dialogue to core values and vital behaviors. Leaders should also make certain that they weigh key goals appropriately relative to one another in evaluating performance. Senior leaders might declare that the patient experience is the most important organizational priority, weighing it at only 10 percent of a team's or individual's total performance score (with other priorities given more weight). Confusion abounds as people dedicate their focus, effort, and time to the more heavily weighted standards. Remember, when transforming culture, you must hold people accountable for upholding the desired culture.

Developing Transformational Leaders

Creating successful transformational leaders requires ongoing learning. Organizations can cultivate their own leaders in-house through internal leadership development programs or partner with third-party organizations like Press Ganey to supply content or guide the process. "Growing your own" crop of leaders can allow you to incorporate company-specific policies and practices into leadership training and groom individuals in customized ways.

To develop high-performing, outcomes-based transformational leaders, begin with your organization's values, the competencies most important for leaders, and your goals for leadership development programming. You might wish to weave these elements into a leadership development mission statement or "philosophy." Rehearse the philosophy at the start of every session or frame it and hang it on the wall in the training room to set the stage, publicly showcasing the training's larger purpose.

The best training programs engage leaders as soon as they're hired or promoted. Share information about what participants must achieve to succeed, and provide necessary resources or support. Press Ganey ensures that new leaders attend a Management 101 course within 30 to 60 days of employment, equipping them with the tools, training, and insight they require. At your organization, such an early orientation could include a company policy overview, interviewing and hiring guidelines, legal aspects of management, "where to find" key resources, and other topics leaders need as they embark on a new role. Avoid assuming that any new leader, regardless of background or experience, understands your organization's specific rules, policies, practices, and procedures. Take advantage of the opportunity to orient new members, recognizing that any investment you make here will pay off over the long term.

New leaders also require ongoing training and development. Ensure that such resources are relevant and realistic in time and scope. Offerings might consist of in-person courses such as an intensive or multiple-day academy, e-learning courses, self-learning modules, or a combination. Avoid onetime educational immersions (sometimes referred to as "dipping") in a topic, as that rarely changes behavior in a meaningful way. Enduring change requires solid, initial training coupled with follow-up and reinforcement in the form of additional in-person training, an online course, a webinar, a self-learning module, or an infographic. This approach is sometimes referred to as *blended learning*, since it positions several approaches on top of one another.[3]

Consider the *style* of training delivery as well. Blended learning, which refers to content delivery across multiple modalities (such as combining in-person training with an online course), is a leadership development best practice approach. While most organizations rely upon in-person, instructor-led training, this is often costly and logistically challenging, especially in large or multistate organizations. E-learning courses, by contrast, allow organizations access to a vast library of potentially relevant and helpful courses. Figure 4.1 showcases a blended learning approach featuring initial in-person training, and annual refresher training, with reinforcement classes interspersed.

Figure 4.1 A "Blended Learning" Approach to Leadership Development

E-learning courses are especially helpful because they allow for the scaling of material into smaller, bite-sized sessions (often referred to as "microlearning"). Some organizations have developed a series of "monthly learning nuggets" in which leaders receive a different single-topic, four-minute mini-course each month, allowing for incremental learning throughout the year. Organizations have also succeeded with virtual learning leadership development events in which an in-person training session is "broadcast" online to sites throughout the country, enabling universal participation. Other resources include 360-degree evaluations, EQ assessments, the use of personality indexes like Myers-Briggs™ or DiSC®, and individual coaching or mentoring.

Conclusion

This chapter has invited you to imagine a healthcare system in which everybody contributes their full potential, engagement is impressive, and leaders understand their roles in fostering and transforming the workforce. We've asked you to consider the impact leaders can have when they cultivate an environment in which exceptional behavior yields exceptional results, exceptional culture drives exceptional behavior, and exceptional leadership fosters an exceptional culture. Challenge yourself to grow and develop as a leader as you practice self-leadership, the leadership of others, and organization-wide transformation. All are critical to providing high-quality care and service to patients and their families. Always remember that if a healthy and fit culture accelerates performance, it's ultimately a special kind of leader who accelerates culture: a transformational one.

IN SUM

- Transactional leadership is a limited approach in which leaders become overly mired in minutiae.
- Transformational leadership is broader, more strategic, and focused on cultural evolution and team engagement.
- Transformational leaders create the culture that influences behavior that produces results.
- Transformational leadership is a threefold proposition that requires leading oneself, leading others, and leading transformation.

Measures, Metrics, and Key Drivers

Kristopher H. Morgan, PhD, and Stephanie B. Weimer, MA

> *Engagement-related metrics serve many functions for leaders, helping them set goals, ensure accountability, and distinguish between good and bad strategies. But you must attend to the quality of your metrics if you are to reach your organizational objectives.*

A LONGTIME PARTNER client of ours recently learned a hard lesson about how vital measurement and metrics are to the success of an organizational transformation initiative. After several years of working with us, the organization decided to discontinue our validated core instrument and use only just-in-time pulse surveying to gather information on engagement. The organization had seen a slight decline in engagement scores and believed that changing the survey design would help catalyze positive change. The organization included survey components (hereafter referred to as "items") designed by their leadership team and various other internal stakeholders. These items were sets of questions they had researched or that struck them as sensible and capable of providing them the data they really needed—items that "got to the underlying issues."

This organization didn't test their homegrown survey before putting it into the field. Six months later, leaders ran into trouble when they attempted to analyze the resultant data and use it to make improvements. The information the survey returned was disparate, and leaders couldn't discern any meaningful patterns. Each question reflected the preconceived notions of the person who devised it, and the totality of these individually constructed items painted a murky, disjointed, and confusing picture. With no clear basis for action, leaders found themselves unable to set clear goals, and analysis paralysis set in.

Anyone can create a survey, and many do-it-yourself survey websites provide tools to do just that. But selecting such a tool begs the question of what you hope to do with the resultant data. If you wish to make improvements, secure buy-in for improvement strategies, and hold others accountable, you must use consistent, valid, and reliable measures. Organizations such as Press Ganey can promise reliable, valid, and actionable data because of their scientifically validated measurement of concepts like engagement and resilience. As we understand, you cannot assume that survey items actually measure important concepts until they are rigorously tested, confirming that measurements are consistent across different types of employees and providers. Our partner organization came to this realization the hard way. Six months after jettisoning our reliable and valid survey, they hastily returned to it.

As we argue in this chapter, using valid and reliable instruments and framing metrics correctly constitutes the foundation of organizational transformation. To help you avoid finding yourself in our partner client's unfortunate situation, we offer a framework you can follow to make strong decisions for improvement, outlining how to use measurement and data to support your strategic plan and your vision for transforming your organization into the best place to work and receive care. We make a simple promise: the engagement measures and metrics we discuss will rely on the best science backed with high-end, psychometric validation. By relying on science, you'll be assured that your data are reliable and yield real benchmarks, that your measures are valid and measure concepts correctly, and that the resultant snapshot of your culture empowers you to make positive change.

Use an Instrument You Can Count On

We've all heard the expression "garbage in, garbage out." This saying holds true for engagement metrics as well. As we saw with the example of our well-meaning partner client, we can always assemble a bunch of survey items and claim that they measure something. But how much do those items and the responses they generate actually reflect reality? The polling companies that predicted the 2016 election thought they were accurately measuring reality, but they mistakenly assumed that they knew what mattered to voters based on past precedent.[1] They didn't properly validate their measurement tools, pilot-testing them to ensure that most people in the population interpreted survey items as they intended. Leaders at healthcare organizations can't afford to make this mistake. We must design, test, and validate surveys across diverse respondents, work units, employee types, and organizations. Only then will we know that our survey tools are accurate.

Proper assessment of an engagement survey includes not merely piloting the survey items, but using psychometric analysis to probe the notion of engagement and distill common elements of employee experience.[2] Assessing for validity (we are measuring what we intend to measure) and reliability (our survey will yield similar results when fielded over different times and among different populations) in a survey instrument is paramount to fulfilling the promises we made at the beginning of this chapter.

When evaluating the validity and reliability of a measurement tool for your organization, you should always ask the following questions:

- Does the survey actually measure engagement and its component parts (something known as "construct validity")? In other words, do the items you selected to represent engagement actually hang together?

- Do the measures that we think contribute to engagement actually contribute to it (something known as "convergent validity")? In other words, are the scores from your engagement measures close enough to converge? "Willingness to recommend a place of work" and "pride," for example, are so closely related that they converge.

- Do the measures we think *aren't* part of engagement truly not contribute to it ("divergent validity")? We must exclude from the engagement measure items that aren't intimately related to engagement, such as "workout facilities at work."

- Does the survey predict outcomes that it, in theory, should predict ("predictive validity")? For instance, if we purport to measure "team attitudes," will that measurement actually predict engagement and other, related concepts?

- Do the survey items consistently measure engagement? That is, do they have "internal consistency reliability"? When we distribute this survey to tens of thousands of healthcare professionals, for example, do we get consistent results regardless of when, where, or to whom it is administered?

- Do the survey items confuse readers because they are written at an overly high level ("readability")? As much as we might not like to admit it, most people don't read consistently beyond an eighth-grade level. Sometimes a survey can contain so much jargon that respondents have trouble interpreting it. This can be the case within even a single organization. We need to use language generic enough that it can be universally interpreted and readily understood.

The response scale also plays a role. Best-in-class measurement systems use Dr. Rensis Likert's 5-point agreement scale to ensure that they can translate your scores into predictive data. (Authors' note: it is actually pronounced LICK-ert, not LIKE-ert, although this is commonly misunderstood.) Like functioning thermostats in your home, Likert scales consistently produce the same results and are easy to read. This means that the psychological distance from a response of 5 ("strongly agree") to a response of 4 ("agree") equals the psychological distance from a response of 1 ("strongly disagree") to 2 ("disagree"). Such considerations might sound trivial, but they mean that you can convert responses into scores that move consistently, differentiate between different subgroups like units or departments, and are easy to understand.

A consistent, psychometrically validated core instrument also helps leaders by defining abstract constructs like "organization," "belonging," "trust," or "respect," and translating them into concrete, stable quantities. We can't measure abstractions directly. As one scholar put it, they represent "a whole complex of beliefs and attitudes."[3] A best-in-class engagement survey assigns each constituent part of engagement a different variable that represents a portion of employee engagement. Survey items thus operate *together* to identify the abstract construct known as "engagement."[4] By using psychometric testing to ensure that metrics reliably measure the intended concepts, organizations obtain better, more consistent measures that allow for more action, intervention, and improvement over time.

Overall, when we think of engagement we mean attachment to, identification with, and involvement in an organization, as measured by concepts such as pride, loyalty, and overall satisfaction. Individual items dealing with these concepts contribute to a psychometrically validated composite engagement score. At Press Ganey, we operationalize our definition of engagement with this score and the following six survey items that comprise it: "I am proud to tell people I work for this organization," "I would stay with this organization if offered a similar job elsewhere," "I would recommend this organization to family and friends who need care," "I would like to be working at this organization three years from now," "I would recommend this organization as a good place to work," and "Overall, I am a satisfied employee."

Do This: Use a standardized core set of survey items, and add items to measure the success of specific initiatives or behavioral changes.

Not That: Don't add items to the survey that are unrelated to specific behaviors you want to change. When employees see a new item on a survey but can't detect any actions taken, they lose faith in the process. Avoid incorporating "pet projects" into standard employee surveying. By including an item, you signal that the organization will act on the result.[5]

The Essential Measures and Metrics

In addition to ensuring the accuracy of measurement tools, leaders must measure the right elements at optimal times to obtain the insights they need to achieve a desired culture. Due to healthcare's complexity, organizations must measure several constituent parts of engagement to obtain a clear picture of the workforce and its feelings. The traditional approach of assessing "employee satisfaction" is insufficient. We must administer culture and engagement surveys to understand where organizations are operating well culturally and where they might improve. Using a survey tool that includes items unique to specific roles (like nursing or physician engagement items), specific causes (like safety culture), or specific trends unfolding inside the organization (like assessing resilience of caregivers) provides organizations with a fuller picture of their organizational culture. Press Ganey provides a "One Ask" survey that includes such elements, prompting only "one ask" of the respondent and collecting insights across several areas that typically require separate surveys. This minimizes survey fatigue and respects respondents' time.

Based on our years of experience, we have identified eight key metrics on which organizations should report findings to understand their culture comprehensively. These include an overall engagement metric that helps us understand the pride that caregivers feel in the organization, a team index to help us understand team functionality and collaboration, and a measure around managers' effectiveness to help us understand the team's perception of its leader. Table 5.1 (see next page) lists these key metrics, along with how Press Ganey defines them. Each metric helps illuminate organizational culture, enabling leaders to identify improvement areas.

In addition to the metrics detailed previously, you should consider including survey items that align with your mission and values, key initiatives, and organizational objectives. Under the auspices of its "Office of Caregiver Experience," Cleveland Clinic formed a cross-functional survey design team involving key stakeholders across the organization to ensure that the items on its survey aligned with organizational objectives and key results (OKRs). One of its caregiver OKRs, for example, is to "Be

Table 5.1   Core Engagement Metrics

Metric/Measure	Definition	Sample Item
Engagement Indicator	Composite metric of six items that measure employees' degree of pride in the organization, intent to stay, willingness to recommend, and overall workplace satisfaction. This score is considered Press Ganey's primary outcome metric.	"I would recommend this organization to others as a good place to work."
Team Index	Measures the level of team functioning and viability. Scores in this index indicate the level of support needed to effectively drive improvement and positive outcomes.	"My work unit works well together."
Leader Index	Measures how well-prepared a work group leader is to manage a work group through activities that support improvement and positive outcomes. This key metric provides insight into leader–employee relationships by measuring trust, respect, communication skills, and openness to discussing issues and solutions.	"I respect the abilities of the person to whom I report."
Physician Alignment	Assesses the extent to which physicians feel a strong partnership and connection with leadership and have a shared vision of how to execute the organizational mission. The alignment metric provides insight into how to improve the relationship between physicians and leadership.	"I have adequate input into decisions that affect how I practice medicine."
Safety Culture Index	Measures individual and group values, attitudes, perceptions, competencies, and patterns of behavior that impact the commitment and ability to provide a safe environment for employees, physicians, and patients. Press Ganey's Safety Culture measure consists of the following: (1) Prevention & Reporting, (2) Resources & Teamwork, and (3) Pride & Reputation.	"I can report patient safety mistakes without fear of punishment."
Resilience	Measures the ability of employees and physicians to recover and remain engaged even in challenging work circumstances, providing an early warning system for burnout. The index is divided into "Activation" and "Decompression." Activation items focus on connection to meaning and purpose, while decompression items focus on employees' ability to disconnect from work.	"I can enjoy my personal time without focusing on work matters."
Nursing Engagement	Assesses nurse engagement and key drivers across the seven American Nurses Credentialing Center (ANCC) nursing satisfaction categories: (1) Autonomy, (2) Professional Development, (3) Leadership Access and Responsiveness, (4) Interprofessional Relationships, (5) Fundamentals of Quality Nursing Care, (6) Adequacy of Resources and Staffing, and (7) RN-to-RN Teamwork and Collaboration.	"Nurse leaders share a clear vision for how nursing should be practiced in this organization."
Diversity & Inclusion	Set of measures that, when used in conjunction with existing core measures, heighten understanding of diversity-related dynamics and help foster an engaged workforce regardless of employee background.	"This organization values employees from different backgrounds."

the Safest Place to Work in Healthcare." Two additional survey items—"Cleveland Clinic cares about employee safety" and "I feel free to raise workplace safety concerns"—convey caregivers' perceptions of their progress toward Cleveland Clinic's ultimate goal of reducing workplace violence. Meanwhile, "Cleveland Clinic provides career development opportunities" and "My manager supports me in developing new skills" allow Cleveland Clinic to evaluate progress toward their OKR to "Be the best place to learn and grow."

Organizations should also consider including items that evaluate employees' appraisal of key organizational changes. Healthcare is experiencing more mergers and acquisitions, large information technology (IT) implementations, leadership reorganizations, and new or refreshed organizational initiatives or programs than ever before. Change brings uncertainty and insecurity, requiring effective communication and visible leadership. Organizations undergoing major change should consider including items that evaluate how employees regard communication, leadership structure, the organization's future vision, and their sense of psychological safety. Organizations might include an item such as "Changes affecting this organization are communicated in a way I can understand" to evaluate the effectiveness of communication regarding the change. They can also run analyses that study the relationships between key areas. Are employees who don't understand a key initiative less engaged than those who do? Do employees who are less enamored of their managers feel the organization is also failing to live up to its mission and values? Creating a single, integrated survey with the relevant items can help answer these and many other interesting questions.

In addition to the scaled items on the survey, open-ended items can shine additional light on the organizational culture, providing qualitative feedback to supplement quantitative data. As a best practice, organizations should include two open-ended, free-text questions on the survey asking for both positive and constructive feedback. An organization might identify career development as one of its key improvement opportunities. Including items like, "What educational experiences have you found to be most valuable in the last year?" and "Please provide one suggestion on how we can better provide career development opportunities for you at our hospital" could help leaders understand whether employees are most interested in professional development, promotion, education, or training, and whether this sentiment varies across the organization.

Do This: Select the right items to measure the full breadth of your organizational culture, including traditional engagement items, job-related items for select groups, and key organizational initiatives. Report the findings through consistent metrics that represent the organization's current state of culture.

Not That: Don't measure "satisfaction" without considering other key elements of culture. Satisfaction alone will offer you a vague, incomplete picture that precludes effective action.

From Metrics to Action

Data alone won't allow an organization to improve engagement. Organizations must also glean meaningful *insights* from the data. The sheer volume of data organizations collect can overwhelm leaders, leading them to waste valuable time. Strategically mining data for insights allows us to focus on significant issues and apply resources intelligently. It also helps leaders and managers craft effective stories to bolster their planning and improvement initiatives.

As a basis for generating insights, leaders should pay close attention to industry benchmarks, allowing them to see how the organization compares to its counterparts. Given the high-stakes nature of healthcare and employees' tendency to regard patient care as a "calling," engagement-related metrics might come in significantly higher than at organizations in other industries. Comparing healthcare to the aerospace or manufacturing industry, for instance, might seem interesting, but doing so might distort or misrepresent the performance benchmarks needed to achieve excellence.

Alongside national benchmarks, focus on item-level or subgroup benchmarks. Absent benchmarks in staffing, for example, organizations might decide to invest heavily in hiring based on a low score alone, not realizing that other organizations are in fact performing well with similar staffing levels, and the low scores owe to inefficient processes. In addition to comparative benchmarks, organizations should look for *key drivers* of engagement and resilience—items in your survey that best predict these outcomes statistically. To identify these drivers and their impact, we use multiple regression analyses. Such analyses help answer the questions, "How can we build a culture of engagement and resilience?" and "Where should I focus my improvement efforts to have the greatest impact on engagement or resilience?"

We recommend using these key drivers, alongside the specific organizational strengths and opportunities indicated by the data, to pinpoint important themes and patterns. Table 5.2 presents key drivers for employee and physician engagement and resilience based on our analysis of national data, listed in order of impact for that metric. As we can see, providing high-quality care and service is the most important factor driving employee engagement, while having confidence that the hospital will succeed in the future is paramount for physicians. In general, this table shows how important it is for employees and physicians to believe in the organization's mission and values, to feel that the organization is patient-focused, and to believe that mutual respect and positive relationships exist. Like benchmarks, these key drivers illuminate insights in the data that can help organizations highlight where to focus and how to secure the biggest return on their time and resource investments.

Table 5.2   National Key Drivers of Engagement and Resilience

Employee	Physician	Resilience
High-quality care and service	Confidence in future success of hospital	Reasonable job stress
Senior management's actions support mission/values	High-quality care and service	Support for work–life balance
Treating employees with respect	Treating physicians with respect	Work gives feeling of accomplishment
Work gives feeling of accomplishment	Satisfaction with recognition	Liking the work
Liking the work	Feeling patients are satisfied with care received	Clear job responsibilities
Environment motivates going above and beyond	Adequate input into decisions	Satisfaction with job security
Respect for manager's abilities	Organization conducts ethical business	Time to provide best care/service
Job makes good use of skills/abilities	Level of collegiality among physicians	Seldom distractions from work
Fairness of pay	Easily communicate ideas/suggestions	Work unit follows proper procedures for customer service
Effort to deliver safe, error-free care	Availability of tools and resources for best care	Work unit effort to deliver safe, error-free care

While national key drivers of engagement and resilience remain fairly consistent over time, new drivers can arise depending on shifts in the state of healthcare. Key drivers for individual organizations can also differ from the national list for many reasons, including differences in workforce and culture and major or disruptive changes that occur in a given year. For this reason, leaders seeking to drive improvement should evaluate the key drivers that exist within their own organization, and not rely solely on national insights. In Chapter 6, we'll provide a comprehensive strategy for using metrics for data segmentation and performance acceleration.

To achieve their business objectives and maximize bottom-line performance, organizations should analyze various data together. Press Ganey's critical metrics map unites the essential metrics that organizations track across workforce, patient experience, and safety. This diagnostic tool provides organizations with an easy way to understand consistency and disconnects across metrics, allowing leaders to shape improvement initiatives more precisely. Press Ganey research has found, for example, an association between stronger workforce and physician engagement and better patient experience scores, shorter lengths of stay, lower rates of hospital acquired infections, and higher financial margins.[6] Our latest research has also uncovered a link between the percentage of high-performing teams (as identified by a team index designation of "1") and Leapfrog safety grade (a widely used measure of patient safety). We also found that facilities that reduced the number of struggling teams (as identified by a team index of "3") by at least 10 percent one year were 1.59 times more likely to improve their safety grade by at least one letter the following year. Similarly, facilities that reduced the number of team index "3" groups by at least 10 percent were 380 percent more likely to improve their "overall rating" percentage by at least 3 percent the following year.[7] These findings support our essential premise: an engaged workforce drives high performance in safety, quality, and patient experience.

Organizations should use workforce metrics in conjunction with other human resources metrics such as turnover, absenteeism, vacancy rates, time-to-fill positions, and performance evaluations. The Medical University of South Carolina (MUSC), a comprehensive academic healthcare system headquartered in Charleston, South Carolina, evaluates engagement alongside turnover data. An analysis revealed that engagement for those who remained with MUSC Health in 2019 had been 64 percentile points higher in 2017 compared to those who had voluntarily left the organization. Those who had stayed with the organization rated their resistance to leave as 0.49 points higher, and their intent to stay with the organization as 0.63 points higher. These are significant differences on a 5-point scale, especially when compared to those employees who voluntarily left. Further analysis revealed that those who had stayed felt more connected to the organization and their team, whereas those who had left were influenced by factors such as job stress, communication, pay, and a desire for meaningful work. MUSC plans to use these findings, alongside their critical metrics map, to refine how they support hiring and onboarding and how they use stay interviews to drive retention.

Do This: When analyzing data, attempt comparisons that make sense, and stick to them. Consider group(s) that are national, regional, and specific to your organization (no more than three) and agree on them. Further, analyze the data for just a few meaningful patterns and insights to guide improvement.

Not That: Stop looking for a "skinny mirror." Everyone wants to look good, but when it comes to forming your comparison group, avoid fishing for benchmarks that make you shine. Also, don't spend countless hours and resources mining the data for the "silver bullet." Many organizations suffer from "analysis paralysis," devoting quality time and resources on myriad data analyses to determine the best course of action. This wastes valuable time and stalls improvement efforts.

Goal Setting and Metric Selection

With the right metrics and insights in hand, organizations must also define meaningful goals for leaders, teams, and the entire organization. Goal setting provides a road map for incremental improvement the organization needs to make to achieve its objectives. Although goal setting can take a number of forms, as other chapters in this book attest, not all goal strategies conform well with certain metrics, and some metrics don't provide the right type of benchmarks to guide improvement.

To avoid common goal-setting pitfalls, organizations should distinguish between *attainment goals* that are framed around achieving a specific target (like a mean score or a percentile ranking), and *achievement goals* designed to assess levels of improvement from one time frame to the next. Goals set around attaining a certain ranking year over year can help with decision-making at the board level, while achievement goals are most conducive for engaging frontline caregivers in improvement initiatives. Both types of goals have their time and place, and leaders should thoughtfully consider each. Although percentile rankings are among the most popular ways to benchmark performance and judge attainment, such rankings have their limitations. So much of ranking involves the performance of others—something beyond our influence. Ranks are fine to follow, but if you really want to fast-track improvement, focus on moving the actual scores.

Partner clients often ask why their rankings fluctuate so dramatically when their score remains unchanged. "It's so frustrating," they say, "because small differences seem to lead to such big changes in ranks. It makes it really hard to keep people focused and I never know what to expect." We point out that rankings can fluctuate dramatically even when the underlying scores remain steady, making it hard for leaders to glean useful insights. Also, percentile ranks are packed very tightly in the database, and small changes in the mean ranking can impact them tremendously. In fact, we suggest, there's a deeper problem here. By linking goals to others' performance, leaders can often feel that they lack control. We advise considering percentile ranks as a supplement to other improvement metrics rather than as *the* major litmus test for your organization. If you continue to increase your mean score, eventually your ranking will increase. Focus most on moving your raw score, whether you're seeking to improve performance in an individual work unit, a division, or an entire organization.

Another question to consider is what *type* of score to use: "mean," "top box," or "percent favorable." A mean score is created by adding up different scores and taking their average. A top box score is the percentage of respondents that gave you the top score on an item, and percent favorable combines the percentage of employees that answered either "agree" or "strongly agree" for an item. We suggest choosing mean scores, since doing so tends to make tracking improvement straightforward.

Let's say that an organization started with a 4.18 mean score and 78 percent favorable responses to the item, "Overall I am a satisfied employee." After the organization implemented a sweeping initiative the following year, its mean score increased to 4.39, yet it still maintained 78 percent favorable responses to that item. If the organization set its goal as "increasing the percent favorable," the organization's confused managers and leaders might be tempted to think, "We improved, but we also stayed the same." In this case, the initiative's success occurred at the lower end (those previously reporting "strongly disagree" moved to "disagree") and/or the upper end (those reporting "agree" moved to "strongly agree"). This didn't show up as a difference in the percent favorable score, since that score compresses the scale into "favorable" and "not favorable" responses—you can't see movement at the edges of the scale.[8] This organization made impressive strides that would sadly go unnoticed if managers focused only on the top of

the scale. Focusing efforts on the lower end of the scale, by contrast, is better because those areas generally correspond with lower
morale, culture breakdowns, and increased prevalence of safety
incidents. No matter where you focus, mean scores are best to use,
as these simple measurements provide you with a full picture of
performance.

Another important consideration when setting goals is to render them realistic and attainable, not aspirational, and to change
them to match the organization's evolving objectives, vision, and
strategic plan. Many organizations might decide to make goals
more or less aggressive based on current priorities and anticipated
future changes. For instance, an organization poised to implement a new electronic health record (EHR) might lighten goals
during the implementation phase, proactively recognizing the stress
that change can produce. This organization isn't "copping out,"
but rather building momentum that can lead to greater employee
engagement in the future. Formulating tiered goals—a threshold
goal that outlines organizations' minimal achievement, a true target
goal, and a "stretch" or aspirational goal—is a useful best practice.

For many organizations, accountability is critical when goal setting. We recommend that organizations start goal-setting efforts
at the system and facility levels, focusing primarily on the engagement indicator metric described previously. As we saw in Chapter 3,
many organizations also decide to set goals at the leader and department levels. While managers play a large role in engaging their staff
and aligning them with the organization's objectives, many of the
factors impacting engagement do not entirely reside within their
control. When setting leader and department goals for engagement,
organizations should thus provide leaders with strong support and
resources to drive change. Organizations should also set goals inde-
pendently for each department based on each group's circumstances.

In lieu of or in addition to asking managers to achieve certain scores, organizations should also consider aligning manager

goals with managerial behaviors known to drive engagement and workforce behaviors.[9] Press Ganey recommends that our partners include the following three yes/no items on pulse surveys to assess such behaviors and hold leaders accountable: (1) "Has your leader shared the most recent employee engagement survey results?", (2) "Were you involved in action planning as a result of the most recent survey?", and (3) "Have you been kept up-to-date about the progress of the action plans?" One leading healthcare organization featured these questions in their midyear pulse survey. The results supported our hypothesis that these leadership behaviors were related to higher engagement, team index, and leader index scores (even for an already high-performing, top-quartile organization like this). Specifically, we found that individuals who answered "yes" to all three items had an average engagement score in the 99th percentile, and a leader index of 95 (a measurement of leadership capability described in Table 5.1—think of a 95 as an "A" grade from school). Further, only 4 percent of these respondents were on teams with the lowest team index of "3." Conversely, those who answered "no" to all three items averaged in the 29th percentile for engagement and had an average leader index score of 73 (think of this as a "C" grade from school). Of these respondents, 67 percent were on teams designated with the lowest team index of "3." These behavioral measures can supplement other monitoring and goal-setting interventions to help determine where efforts fall short, and if noncompliance with these behaviors is an issue.

A final consideration around goal setting concerns incentives. Many organizations incent leaders to prioritize and focus efforts on driving improvement. Monetary incentives, however, can have negative effects, making the survey more about judgment than improvement. They can also create silos within organizations, encourage unethical behavior, and stymie innovation efforts as leaders focus unduly on achieving a predetermined score.[10] For these reasons, we suggest exercising great caution when developing incentive plans around workforce survey scores.

If you feel the need to incent people, start at the senior leadership level and base goals on the performance of each leader's entire team. Cascade the goals so that everyone on the team works toward the same objective(s) and either receives the incentive together or not at all. Another best practice when using monetary incentives is to rank engagement and workforce goals as a small percentage of the total possible incentive, with the rest determined by key business objectives such as patient experience, safety, productivity, performance, and so on. This method is more holistic, ensuring that any one metric doesn't monopolize the others. Finally, consider whether nonmonetary incentives like awards, praise, and other formal recognition will suffice to motivate improvement. For employees and leaders in the healthcare industry, the return on investment achieved from building a culture of engagement is often incentive enough.

Do This: Set achievement goals that people and teams can attain incrementally. Break down achievement into smaller, reasonable "chunks," and check in frequently to determine whether people are attaining these goals. By "chunking" long-term goals, you can more easily secure buy-in for each piece. Staff have a far easier time committing to make several small, shorter-term changes than they do to making one big, longer-term change. This strategy also allows you to reward individuals and teams incrementally, keeping people aligned and focused.

Not That: Don't expect too big of an improvement in one survey cycle. "I know we are in the 37th percentile," a manager might say, "but as an organization we want to be in the 90th percentile by next year." Although common, such excessively high expectations can result in frustration, anxiety, and eventually, abandonment of the goal. Not all work groups or facilities start in the same place. Some have further to go and will take longer to get there. The fastest way to deflate team morale is to set unrealistic goals.

Measure What Matters

When it comes to efforts to improve culture and employee engagement, the quality of your measurement really does make a profound difference. You can certainly use homegrown surveys to track how your people feel about their work and the organization—many organizations do. But very few succeed in improving engagement and culture in significant ways and sustaining those gains over time. If you don't use validated survey instruments, your improvement initiative will lack clearly defined benchmarks and reliable checkpoints for improvement. Key stakeholders will have no way of distinguishing between good and bad strategies, or between areas where improvement had occurred and areas where it hadn't. At the organization described in the beginning of this chapter, leaders' initial examination of data set off a firestorm of emails and contentious meetings about what went wrong. Such conflict further distracted from improvement efforts, derailing their transformation until the next survey cycle, when they returned to the core instrument.

Don't make a similar mistake. With this chapter's frameworks and best practices in hand, you can drive changes in behavior that will have a lasting impact on your organization and its people.

IN SUM

- Organizations that bypass science when settling on measurement instruments are making a profound mistake. Unless the measurement tool selected is both valid and reliable, it might not provide directional insights that will drive change.
- Choose a survey that you can count on, and stick with it. Use a standardized core set of survey items, and add items to measure the success of specific initiatives or behavioral changes.
- Measurement without action causes "inaction fatigue." To avoid this, only capture insights on items around which you intend to act. Focus your improvement efforts on meaningful patterns identified from those data.
- Be thoughtful about goal setting, choosing metrics, benchmarks, incentives, and goals that are real and attainable. Leaders and caregivers must be able to see meaningful differences in day-to-day activities as well as in the metrics to know that change is happening.

Building Data Plans to Drive Improvement

David Shinsel

> *To use data effectively, healthcare organizations must prepare for it. Although they can sharpen and define some elements more precisely once they receive data insights, high-performing organizations proactively establish goals, boundaries, and structures for their data usage. This chapter discusses how organizations can build plans for using data, thus avoiding common pitfalls.*

"I CAN'T FIND my buddy," the panicked diver said, "and I'm low on air!" It was the fall of 2006, and my younger brother Andy and I, both SCUBA instructors, were working on a chartered boat anchored near Catalina Island, California. In a matter of seconds, we gathered information from the diver, discussed our plan, and plunged into the water to begin our search for the missing partner. After some time, our search pattern led us to a disoriented diver who was critically low on oxygen and in dangerously deep water. After confirming that he was okay, we grabbed his buoyancy compensator (the harness holding divers' air tanks) to prevent him from becoming separated from us or ascending too quickly. We calmed him down, provided him with auxiliary air, and guided him safely to the surface.

During the debrief that followed, we learned that this pair of divers made several mistakes, but most critically, they failed to develop a dive plan. They jumped in without a common understanding of where they'd go, how long they'd stay, and how they'd communicate. When one diver spotted a lobster scrambling to find a new hiding spot in the coral, he lost his partner in the swaying shadows cast by curtain-like ribbons of a kelp forest that protruded several stories high from the ocean floor. The two were hardly rookies, but their failure to create and execute a plan nearly ended in tragedy.

Organizations embarking on cultural improvement efforts make similar mistakes when it comes to their data. They might have general ideas for how to improve their culture, but instead of planning their data use in advance, they wait for the data to appear and then build their plans afterward. The results aren't nearly as pretty as a kelp forest. At some organizations, leaders become so fixated on uncovering exotic data stories and mapping out every possible relationship between metrics that they struggle to build momentum for improvement. At other organizations, confusion reigns. I once worked with an organization that gathered cultural feedback only because other organizations did so. Leaders didn't seem to know why they were gathering data or what they'd do once they amassed it. As data flowed in, the human resources (HR) team in charge of surveying employees tried to process the information even as they responded to leaders' calls for immediate action. Change efforts floundered, and when the organization failed to take action, survey participants felt ignored. The organization lost any return on the investment in cultural listening they had made, and enthusiasm for future efforts eroded.

Leaders can achieve much better outcomes with a bit of advance planning. This chapter will present a series of steps organizational leaders should take when planning how to use data so that their efforts to improve culture and engagement succeed. By avoiding common pitfalls and considering the boundaries and structures for leveraging data effectively, leaders can make the most of data, using it to drive much needed change for employees and patients.

Before You Start, Beware the Pitfalls

As other chapters in this book demonstrate, data play a critically important role in the improvement process. Much like signal flares can indicate important events, data can call attention to important stories by highlighting trends and noteworthy disparities within an organization. Data can also confirm issues leaders know about and shed light on those they don't, sparking questions and dialogue. Data can serve as a gauge for measuring progress, and can help leaders discern relationships between key metrics that are critical to organizational goals. None of this is to suggest that the role of data is fixed. On the contrary, data's role must evolve as your organization changes if it is to help your organization further its goals.

But be sure to place limits to how data are used. Organizational excellence and dysfunction typically manifest as complex interactions and relationships. Singular data points should therefore never serve as a leader's only source of understanding, much less determine action. Leaders who confuse immediate reactions to data fluctuations with strategy do so at their peril. Likewise, don't think of data as a key that will magically unlock the secrets to cultural transformation. Some organizations fall for this siren song and believe that if they just dig deep enough within their data, they'll uncover a single solution capable of changing everything. Cultural change is difficult, making the search for supposedly hidden insights and groundbreaking approaches alluring. Unfortunately, these pursuits often delay action and accountability.

Just as survey metrics represent somewhat distant translations of individual perceptions, goals such as achieving a certain score or rank represent distant translations of the true goals of safety, quality, patient-centricity, and cultural excellence.

Misinterpreting data's fundamental role is not the only mistake organizations make when trying to leverage data for improvement. Leaders often interpret data incorrectly by bending metrics to purposes for which they are ill-suited. One organization believed that all managers needed to create improvement plans to raise the organization's overall engagement index score. And yet, the engagement metric isn't designed to drive team-level action, as it deals with big-picture outcomes of the employee experience—like pride and willingness to recommend—that team leaders can't readily influence (for information on data metrics and their differing utility, see Chapter 5).[1] Likewise, key drivers represent items with the greatest statistical impact on outcome metrics like engagement at an organizational level, but they might not comprise the most critical improvement areas for a specific team. Local teams might find that unit-level metrics that don't bear on the organization as a whole reveal the most tangible opportunities for improvement. And some struggling teams might cue into even more specific themes or items that impact their local improvement journey.

Understanding how and in what circumstances to best use these various data points can enhance your strategic improvement plan and increase your odds of success. Organizations that build highly effective plans enlist their leadership teams to choose the engagement and safety measure metrics that belong on their scorecards. They ensure that leaders understand how to use metrics that indicate where teams need support, and they give local teams guidance on how to decide where to take action.

Unfortunately, leaders sometimes emphasize singular scores instead of looking for the picture that emerges in larger *patterns* of data. Several years ago, an organization I worked with became fixated on improving a key driver dealing with the extent to which caregivers felt respect from the organization. Leaders' knee-jerk reaction was to start building plans to emphasize collegiality across their organization, because that is how they interpreted "respect." Thankfully, more thoughtful members of the data team noticed a pattern of low scores around related items dealing with career development opportunities, compensation, and responsiveness to feedback. After reading some verbatim comments, they learned that the larger pattern concerned significantly more than just peer-to-peer collegiality.

An organization's key driver item might seem important for engagement based on statistical analysis, but if other related items show lagging scores, there is likely a larger phenomenon at play. Additionally, one survey item might perform on par with benchmarks at the organizational level, but if an entire department or job category within the organization struggles in that area, the data may again reveal a meaningful story. Leaders who only pay attention to mean scores instead of considering national benchmarks, percentages of favorable or unfavorable responses, and historical comparisons can also fail to spot meaningful data patterns. As you review your data, identify what high- and low-performing items have in common, and search for patterns as you focus on next steps.

Aside from determining how to use data points effectively, some organizations are overly rigid in how they interpret what metrics or items might mean for caregivers. A score on a survey can indicate an opportunity for improvement, but matching the data story with the appropriate actions requires a nuanced understanding of what caregivers had in mind when they provided data. As in our previous example, some survey participants might perceive items dealing with respect as related to collegiality and professionalism, while others might link them to advancement opportunities and compensation. Both perspectives revolve around the general concept of respect, but the actions necessary to improve each are different. We must acknowledge such limitations and treat data as starting points for understanding instead of prescriptive diagnostics.

In acknowledging that items hold different meanings for different people, organizations should resist efforts to rigidly define how raters conceptualize cultural questions. I once worked with a health system interested in improving confidence in senior management's leadership. As efforts began, debate centered on the individuals whom frontline workers defined as "senior management" when rating. For a brief period, these conversations devolved into arguments about how to better define "senior management" for staff so that they "got it right" in their next survey cycle. Thankfully, this organization soon abandoned such debates, focusing instead on how best to *improve* confidence in senior leadership. Regardless of whom staff had in mind, organizational leaders wanted to address shared concerns. By shifting their focus toward action, the healthcare organization identified consistent steps leaders could take, regardless of whether staff included the chief executive officer (CEO) or their department manager in their personal definitions of "senior management."

Establish the Context and Cause

Beyond knowing how best to deploy your metrics, your organization's data action plan must also consider how to identify the "stories" that metrics reveal. Leaders often take simplicity to excess. They spot a score or data point and jump directly to action because they are convinced they understand the issues underlying the data. But they haven't defined how they'll transition from seeing the data's signal flares to taking appropriate action. In the book *Managing the Unexpected*, Karl E. Weick and Kathleen M. Sutcliffe suggest that one trait highly reliable organizations share is a "reluctance to simplify."[2] Such organizations don't rely on past experience or "common sense" to understand the causes, context, or appropriate courses of action for present circumstances. Likewise, when using data to drive improvement, we should remember that every data point reflects human stories with often complex causes. Just because some of the stories appear familiar or relatable doesn't mean we understand them. To build effective plans for leveraging data, we should seek to understand the nuances that could help us chart a path for effective improvement.

Several years back, while facilitating conversations with physician leaders across multiple departments, a department chair noticed that his physicians gave low ratings for a survey question dealing with "opportunities for continuing medical education." This leader quickly assured our consulting team that he had experienced this before in another department, and that the score reflected a low budget allocated for travel to conferences and workshops. After speaking with physicians ourselves, we learned that team members felt they possessed valuable expertise thanks to their unique training and experiences, but lacked opportunities to share what they knew. Travel wasn't the issue, nor was the desire to learn new skills—these physicians just wanted a venue for imparting their knowledge. If this organization hadn't committed itself in advance to illuminating the *context* behind the data through conversations with the physicians themselves, this leader might have invested in the wrong solution, or worse, completely dismissed the problem as "beyond his control."

Oversimplification can also occur in connection with performance metrics. Low ratings don't necessarily indicate a poor "performing" team. Rather, they might arise when a committed team runs up against inadequate resources, broken processes, leadership failures, or countless other challenges. Imagine a team of information technology specialists tasked with implementing a new electronic medical records system across an organization. After several grueling weeks, the team loses a few key members to attrition and external recruitment. The remaining team members work long hours but struggle to keep up with user needs. They ask for support and resources, but no changes materialize. Eventually, they find themselves trying to survive the implementation project and serve internal stakeholders. Surveyed in this state, this team might register low scores in their survey feedback. And yet, a leader who labels these team members as "low performers" would be dramatically oversimplifying, treating the team as a problem to be solved instead of as a group doing its best to cope. Leaders misinterpreting in this way would inflict additional damage, punishing teams for calling attention to problems in their work.

Data can point toward disengaged or poor-performing teams, but leaders shouldn't draw conclusions based on scores alone. They must deploy a thoughtful verification process that considers the scores' context and causes. Committing to understanding prior to action must be a part of your data plan if you want to translate numbers and stories into meaningful action. Decide in advance who will collaborate with teams and how you'll understand improvement opportunities from the team's point of view. This often requires not only asking managers to work with their teams, but enlisting third parties to facilitate conversations in a safe and confidential environment.

Boundaries and Priorities

After planning how to understand data stories, we must establish appropriate boundaries for data analysis. Too many organizations analyze data endlessly, struggling to transition to action. They search for advanced analytics and complex relationships to understand improvement opportunities, pursuing overly complicated and nuanced insights before addressing more fundamental issues. By chasing exotic data stories through increasingly complicated statistical analyses, these organizations delay their own improvement.

At one organization, qualitative and quantitative data clearly suggested that employees felt dissatisfied with senior leaders' responsiveness to a major operational issue. While leadership initially tried to understand where the greatest challenges lay, they soon fell into the trap of chasing data. Their focus drifted, and they performed analysis after analysis, creating multiple statistical models in attempts to map every possible relationship. Ultimately, these leaders became stuck and had great difficulty taking action. Had they established a boundary for how deeply they'd analyze data prior to focusing on their responsiveness to caregivers, they would have spent their time more efficiently. Instead, they pursued the equivalent of sophisticated engine diagnostics while overlooking the flat tire.

Advanced analytics can help, but only after you cover the basics. You can help your organization establish reasonable boundaries and avoid moving too quickly to advanced data analysis and cutting-edge approaches by considering what we might call "organizational staging"—knowing when to pursue deep or sophisticated insight, and when to focus more simply on building a foundation for execution. To avoid searching too deeply, determine at the outset where you are in the improvement life cycle and align your data strategy accordingly. Organizations that manage average or even above-average performance typically have basic culture building to do, and they often gravitate prematurely to unraveling complicated data stories. The quantity and complexity of data analysis organizations pursue should remain somewhat proportional to how far along they are in executing on the fundamentals (Figure 6.1). After establishing a strong foundation and attaining higher levels of performance, organizations can benefit from analyzing complex relationships and deploying novel methodologies.

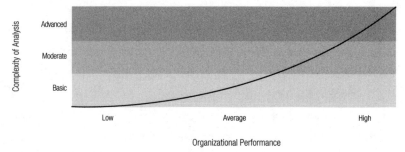

Figure 6.1   Conceptual Relationship Between Organizational Performance and Appropriate Complexity of Analysis

In addition to evaluating organizational staging, you can help establish boundaries for deeper analysis by considering how much additional context exists for a given topic. If department leaders wish to understand team perceptions of respect, they can certainly analyze data to determine whether distinct groups perceive they are respected, and they can explore whether other metrics connect with such perceptions. But they'll likely glean more specific and actionable information by sitting down and talking with their teams. This can happen in a matter of minutes, without developing a complicated analytic model. When such direct sources for contextual understanding aren't unavailable (when leaders are reviewing external data sources, for example, or when they find concerns broadly spread across an organization), then it makes more sense to examine deeper data relationships. But don't jump to that conclusion. Whenever possible, plan in advance for opportunities to go directly to the source.

Another way to help avoid overly complex analysis is to define your data priorities at the outset. When building a culture in healthcare, professional development and team building are important, but safety and care quality issues are preeminent. Improving staff recognition can't take precedence over addressing bullying or other immediately toxic and harmful behaviors. Some of the most inspiring organizations I've worked with have chosen to forgo campaigns or other programming because they're focused on their top goal of pursuing Zero Harm. Spending some time considering your non-negotiables and using them to establish an "order of operations" for certain data stories can help you develop guidelines for prioritization.

Figure 6.2 evokes what an order of operations might look like. The model isn't meant to be overly rigid or comprehensive, but simply to serve as a reference point. For most organizations, data related to culture indicate multiple, legitimate opportunities for improvement. Limiting focus to fewer action areas and establishing a hierarchy of priorities helps leaders answer the question, "Are we focusing on the right topics to achieve our goals?"

Figure 6.2   Sample Order of Operations for Data Topic Prioritization

When establishing an order of operations for data prioritization, healthcare organizations should first identify stories and themes that impact safety and safety culture. Next, identify where employees might harbor negative views of leaders, and focus on "hot spots" within the organization (struggling teams, specific demographic groups, or job families) where the data point to significant challenges. You can then devise strategies for improving organizational and inter/intra team communications, focusing on the processes and resources required to enable teams to optimize productivity and harmony and to eliminate avoidable sources of stress. If no higher-order opportunities exist, identify stretch or developmental opportunities. You can tailor your order of operations to match organizational realities, but it should form part of your plan before you receive data. Debates will inevitably arise about where to invest time and energy, and clarity on priorities at the outset will assist in the decision-making process.

Aside from adopting a general framework for prioritizing certain topics, leaders should pay attention to the intensity of a data message. Some data stories are particularly loud. Instead of admitting your organization scores below average on teamwork, say that 55 percent of all respondents feel that teamwork is poor. Other quantitative examples might include cases in which a given metric is significantly different from benchmarks, receives mostly unfavorable responses, or has dropped significantly. In scenarios like these, staff are forcefully communicating areas of dissatisfaction, and leaders must act. On the other hand, an item may be a key driver, but if it is performing in an acceptable range, consider first addressing more pressing items.

Even if some topics are daunting and difficult, ignoring intense messages can erode confidence and lead caregivers to believe that leaders don't pay attention to their feedback. If leaders spend too much time dissecting and searching for deep explanations to intense messages, employees can perceive them as attempting to deflect responsibility. I've had the unfortunate experience of sitting in an audience of caregivers from across an organization as leaders discussed a range of recent survey results, even though pay fairness was the most glaring and intense message. Leaders felt that since they couldn't give people the salaries they wanted, they were better off avoiding the issue. In truth, the decision to ignore this intense message left the team feeling deflated and patronized, eroded their trust in management, and likely delayed cultural improvement by several years.

Structural Preparation

Another key topic an effective data plan addresses is how best to leverage data when driving change. Leaders must mobilize key players and internal support teams, and ensure proper communications once data become available and actionable. Consider the MRI machine, a miracle of modern science allowing for deep investigation into hidden tissues and structures within the body. This marvel of medical science is useless without someone to operate it and interpret the images it creates. Similarly, you can create an elegant data plan for improvement, but you must also execute it well—specifying who is going to obtain and interpret the data—if it is to have any positive effect.

As research into more than 1,000 organizations revealed, active, visible sponsorship is the most important factor determining a change management effort's success, with effective sponsors claiming triple the success rate over their ineffective sponsorship counterparts.[3] These data match our own experience with healthcare organizations. Organizations in which senior leaders personally use engagement data and help create and execute their strategy outperform organizations that invest culture efforts in teams that lack authority to make decisions or hold others accountable. Working with a large integrated health system, I recently observed that some of the system's hospitals made greater improvements than others. When I asked a team of HR business partners how their hospital had improved so impressively, they noted that their senior leaders "get in the weeds and participate in the culture work." Even the best practices for improvement can fail when they aren't implemented effectively, and there is no substitute for having senior leaders involved and actively using data.

After engaging senior leaders in the change effort, define the internal teams and resources you'll leverage to support improvement work. Leaders and work groups sometimes need help to drive change. It's disheartening when organizations create great plans on paper but lack the teams and resources to translate them into results. Thinking through the groups you'll mobilize to support leaders and teams, as well as the skill-building programs, accountability structures, and coaching resources you'll deploy, can help prevent the stall-outs and false starts that occur when organizations try to define these resources too late. And how will you govern improvement work? Will local teams and leaders really execute well on their own? Does your organization have the resources it needs? Do you know what you're doing, or do you need experts to help? Considering these questions in advance will allow you to put in place the personnel and other resources you'll need to appropriately allocate data among organization members, and support teams based on what the data reveal.

A final structural element to consider in advance has to do with how to convey data. Your data-use plan should physically map out how communications will flow from the top down and bottom up. One organization I worked with mapped out how they'd communicate about data and the actions they'd take well before fielding their cultural survey. They created a clear plan for how to convey results, how they'd articulate expectations for gathering understanding prior to action, and how often they'd track progress on the improvement plan. This team rightly realized that it wouldn't be enough to merely report on how many teams were engaged in improvement efforts; they needed to communicate the quality of efforts team leaders were making as well. This level of structural planning for data and communications enabled this organization to detect drift or identify where teams were failing. It created a closed-loop system in which all leaders understood what was happening, and importantly, how they could modify their approach when necessary. Continuous improvement depends on regular, ongoing messaging around improvement priorities, so that leaders can identify issues and concerns quickly and take corrective action.

While all organizations benefit from evaluating structural preparation, it's even more important for large, complex health systems. There, leaders must account for both system- and local-level functions and their interactions. Such preparation doesn't happen automatically or without continued oversight and (re)calibration. Absent advance preparation, organizations see uneven execution. Leaders shouldn't strictly mandate everything, but in general they should vet and align plans across the organization.

Planning for Work-Unit Triage

In every cultural improvement effort, a certain number of frontline teams struggle to improve and adapt. Sometimes the unit's leader fails to buy in, other times teams feel overloaded with daily work. Whatever the reason, organizations don't typically see improvements if they fail to provide support for these struggling teams. To remedy this problem, data usage plans should specify unit-level measurements, including indicators for teams dealing with inefficient processes, poor team dynamics, and leader–team conflict. Plans should also identify any supplementary actions these teams should take. By first outlining the metrics to classify teams in distress or at risk for safety events, organizations can design triage strategies that match teams with unique resources and guidance.

Just as organizations should commit to understanding the context behind scores, so work-unit triage strategies should emphasize the unit context. After senior leaders leverage team-focused metrics to review and classify teams in need of support, they'll likely have preliminary knowledge of these teams' histories, strengths, and potential barriers to success. To round out this knowledge, they should ask a number of questions to understand the team's state: Has this team experienced a major change in leadership, or work processes? Do any leaders, especially new ones, exhibit any skill or experience gaps? What unique challenges or barriers does this team face? What should we know about the history of this group? Has this team and/or leader bought in to cultural improvement efforts? All of these questions should appear in the formal data plan. Should leaders lack certainty on any of these questions, make provisions for them to gather additional information through conversation and observation.

When organizations have determined how to use work-unit metrics and how to obtain contextual understanding, they can create a visual plan for how they'll support struggling teams. Figure 6.3 presents a template for organizing support activities and evaluating resource needs once data become available. As the figure suggests, work-unit-focused metrics help leaders determine expectations for action and consider unit-level needs. The template highlights where development and coaching might prove necessary, and where teams are staged for self-guided success. It also helps leaders identify critical instances in which they should dig in to obtain additional context on emerging problems. Creating a visual triage template helps sponsors assess resources at their disposal and provide additional support, training, and external assistance.

Building and Activating Your Plan

With the preceding elements in place, leaders can build formal plans to drive improvement once data become available. Begin the process of translating concepts into a plan by identifying the senior leader who will sponsor improvement work and decide how to use organizational data. Don't automatically default to the CEO. Whoever the sponsor is, he or she should feel passionately about the work and willingly assume personal accountability. The most powerful sponsors use their influence to persuade other

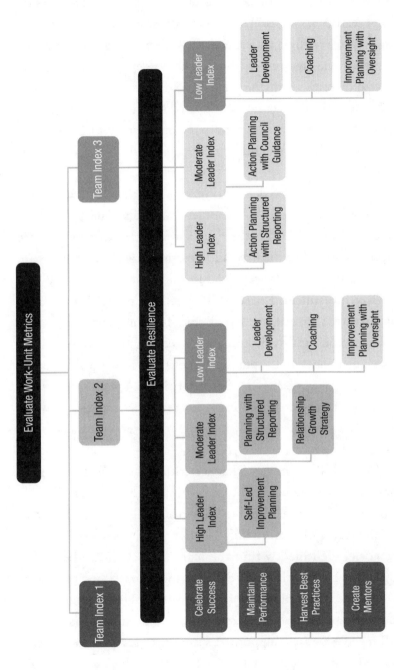

Figure 6.3 Visual Work-Unit Triage Strategy

senior leaders to participate. In building the data usage plan, senior leaders must build agreement on scorecard metrics, indicators for struggling teams, and the order of operations for data prioritization. The sponsor should help leaders work across functions to determine which data points to track, which boundaries will govern the data analysis, and what safeguards are in place to prevent excessive focus on conflicting or redundant improvement activities. Sponsors should also define processes for accountability and calibration.

Leaders must also define the critical problems or "cases" that might arise from data at the team level and determine appropriate remedies for each. Define these cases by referring to your "order of operations" for data priority, and determine as a leadership team which unit-level situations require the most urgent action and resource investment. I once worked with an organization whose top priority was patient safety. Before fielding their survey, they discussed the data stories they were seeking (low safety culture scores, evidence of burnout, and so on) and how they'd support each. Since they discussed their priorities in advance, they were better positioned to make cases for resource investment when needed because they already had convinced senior leaders of the need to take action.

When HR teams can reference critical cases identified in the data plan, they are better able to secure resources as data become available. Instead of trying to convince leaders why to invest in specific teams, they need only identify which teams fall into the categories identified within the plan, and return to the shared goals the plan identifies. To enhance the plan further, turn critical case and unit support decisions into a visual triage strategy that outlines expectations for team actions and indicates which teams will receive focused support. A visual map for how to act upon data can build alignment and make expectations more transparent. It also helps prevent leaders from using low scores punitively.

When teams and leaders know how they'll be supported and what is expected of them based on the data stories that emerge, they'll better understand the motives behind any actions they're asked to take, instead of feeling singled out.

As an extension of the unit triage strategy, your data usage plan should prepare leaders to share what they know about teams once work-unit-focused metrics become available. Develop a list of context- and history-focused questions for each category defined in your critical case as well as the triage map decisions that will help you understand the unique dynamics and challenges at play. Establish expectations for work group leaders to review data with their teams and solicit feedback on improvement solutions. Consider how to leverage focus groups and listening sessions for deeper insight. Challenge leaders to determine if they are oversimplifying issues or acting prematurely. Be transparent about why teams receive assistance and consistently align efforts to organizational goals.

Based on your triage strategy and processes for gaining contextual understanding, determine what internal personnel are available to support struggling teams. Compare internal capabilities, capacity, and expertise, and determine if you'll need additional resources. I've seen well-intentioned HR members identify teams within their organizations in need of urgent support, but instead of mobilizing resources, they find themselves making the case to leadership for why these teams need special attention. In these cases, organizations have failed to consider resource needs as an integral part of their data strategy. If you decide upon resource allocation strategies in the beginning, you won't have to scramble later on to line up support for struggling teams.

With a comprehensive data plan in place, you're now in a position to activate it when data become available. As metrics and stories unfold, incorporate them into your preestablished framework. Revisit your ground rules and agreements, and continuously challenge other leaders to either adhere to the plans or present a well-reasoned argument for adjusting them. Meet with support teams to discuss what they've learned from the data and what information is still missing. Begin to apply your work-unit triage strategy to align resources to teams. As plans are activated and teams are mobilized, communicate, audit execution, and drive accountability.

Conclusion

In recent years, leaders at UF Health Shands Hospital developed an action plan for mobilizing their engagement data. Their most senior leaders personally sponsored the work, executed a data-driven strategy for supporting local teams, and invested financially in the strategy. Their proactive approach allowed them to move quickly and deliberately to drive cultural change. The fruits of their planning and execution have been incredible: nearly a decade of uninterrupted continuous improvement and top-quartile performance in workforce engagement. Your organization can accomplish what UF Health Shands has achieved: to be positioned to proactively leverage data for improvement. If you invest in planning, you'll avoid some of the many common pitfalls that bedevil organizations, and be better able to fulfill your promise of safe, high-quality, patient-centered care. So take to heart the simple advice I always share as my divers prepare to enter the water: "Plan your dive and dive your plan."

IN SUM

- While your data should indicate noteworthy trends, key messages, and topics worth investigating, don't take it as a source of complete understanding.
- Some of the common pitfalls in leveraging data for improvement include failing to understand the uses and interpretation of metrics, failing to consider context and causes behind data, failing to set boundaries and priorities, and a lack of structural preparation for action and support. Planning, communication, and resource investments can help overcome these pitfalls.
- Developing a visual strategy for work-unit triage can help organize support efforts, clarifying expectations and matters of governance.
- Through intentional efforts led by senior leader sponsors, organizations can create comprehensive plans for leveraging data that help them maximize improvement and prevent drift.

7 | Nursing Engagement

Christina Dempsey, DNP, MSN, CNOR, CENP, FAAN, and Mary Jo Assi, DNP, RN, NEA-BC, FAAN

> *Nurses comprise the largest segment of healthcare workers, and they interact most directly with patients. As such, nurses profoundly influence both organizational culture and patient experience. This chapter explains why efforts to improve culture and patient experience require a stable corps of skilled, engaged nurses, and why those nurses must be dedicated to the delivery of safe, high-quality, patient-centered care.*

IT'S SAD BUT true: the healthcare industry is failing to meet nurses' social, emotional, and professional needs. And as a growing body of evidence suggests, this deficit is leading to high rates of job dissatisfaction, disengagement, burnout and, all too often, flight from the profession.[1]

Beth (not her real name), a young registered nurse (RN), knew firsthand about these problems. After spending a year working the night shift as a float nurse in the critical care unit of a busy academic medical center, she was thrilled to accept a full-time position as a critical care nurse. She anticipated that caring for some of the hospital's sickest patients would be challenging, but she felt drawn to trauma medicine. As a nursing student, she had been completing a medical-surgical rotation at a Boston teaching hospital when the 2013 marathon bombing took place. She saw firsthand the difference that skilled, compassionate nurses could make in the lives of critically ill patients. "The way the teams came together and went above and beyond to meet patients' needs was inspiring," she said. "I was moved by the camaraderie and shared sense of purpose, and it was something I hadn't really experienced as a float nurse. I knew working in critical care would be tough, but I definitely felt up for the challenge."

Stepping into her new job, Beth was surprised and chagrined to discover that she couldn't give patients the time and attention they deserved given the sheer amount of work she had to do. "Every day," she said, "I felt this internal struggle. Even though I wanted to do more for my patients—sit with them, talk with them, make them feel cared for and cared about—there just wasn't the time. I felt like I was giving them the bare minimum, when I wanted to give them the maximum. It's so demoralizing to go to work every day knowing you're going to feel like a failure by the end of your shift."

The occasional toxicity of Beth's work environment only compounded her turmoil. "My nurse manager was running in so many different directions that she often couldn't provide direction or support," Beth said. The nurses themselves also seemed to lack cohesiveness and camaraderie. "There didn't seem to be a 'we're in this together' mentality," she said, noting that some of the longer-tenured nurses made it very clear that they didn't have the time or desire to help new nurses. "I had heard about bullying and incivility among nurses, but I honestly didn't believe that was really a 'thing' until I experienced it firsthand."

Adding to her stress, Beth's 12-hour shifts often stretched an hour or two longer because of extra administrative tasks, staffing shortages, and the unpredictability of patient needs. Beth was chronically tired, irritable, and short-tempered with friends and family, and she became increasingly insecure about her caregiving skills. She also had trouble finding meaning in her work. "I never thought the work would be easy, but I did expect it to be rewarding. When I was able to connect with patients and care for them the way I wanted to, the way they deserved, I felt good about it, but more often, I felt like I was coming up short, and I hated that feeling." Less than a year into her job, Beth resigned.

In many ways, the conditions that define today's nursing landscape create a "perfect storm" for disengagement and burnout. Fortunately, most nurse disengagement drivers represent modifiable risk factors—that is, we can fix them. In particular, leaders must use survey tools and other instruments to measure and better understand nurse engagement and job satisfaction, identifying and prioritizing improvement opportunties. After all, robust data and advanced analytics are only valuable if they inspire action and drive improvement. This chapter presents proven strategies that nurse and human resources (HR) leaders can use to transform nursing insights into meaningful improvement.

Recognizing Barriers to Nurse Engagement

Let's look more closely at why so many nurses feel disengaged. It starts with shifts in nursing education. Historically, nursing students spent at least half their time practicing bedside skills on patients and their peers. They gave one another shots, administered IVs, provided head-to-toe assessments, and gave bed baths and backrubs. Hands-on training helped student nurses learn how to connect with their patients, understand their environment, and assess physical and psychosocial needs and suffering. Students supplemented such practical, hands-on training with academic curricula in pharmacology, chemistry, biology, anatomy, and physiology.

Today, much education in the healthcare sciences takes place not with people, but with high-fidelity mannequins that "breathe" and show changes in vital signs. Those mannequins don't cry, experience anger, or react unpredictably or even violently as flesh-and-blood patients might when frightened, in pain, or impaired. Further, thanks to advances in medicine and the shift toward ambulatory, home-based care, many of today's students haven't been hospitalized themselves, nor have they accompanied a close family member through hospital care. As a result, these students feel less comfortable with and adept at face-to-face interactions, a situation amplified by the unfortunate misconception that nurses and other caregivers should distance themselves from patients as a way to mitigate compassion fatigue. The increasing reliance on virtual communication has also changed the way individuals interact and form interpersonal relationships, both of which are foundational to effective nursing practice. It's a recipe for disengagement and burnout.

Ironically, the same medical advances that are improving patients' health and keeping sick patients alive longer can also indirectly influence nurse engagement because patient care needs have become much more complex. Many of today's surgical unit patients would have occupied ICU beds 20 years ago. Patients live longer with chronic diseases like heart failure, chronic obstructive pulmonary disease (COPD), complications of diabetes, and renal failure, increasing the complexity of care as well as that of ongoing nurse education and training. Lengths of hospital stays have diminished, meaning that patients leave the hospital with more complex needs requiring extensive patient education and follow-up. And while many of these complex needs are now being treated in the ambulatory environment, either in clinics or at home, most nursing education programs still focus on acute and inpatient care environments. This discrepancy between training and the reality of care delivery leaves many nurses feeling overwhelmed and stressed.

Shift duration constitutes another important threat to nurse satisfaction and engagement. The 12-hour shift is supposedly the norm. But as was the case for Beth, many of these shifts stretch longer because of administrative burdens. Although many nurses favor the flexibility that longer shifts provide because they can work fewer days, research has consistently linked long shifts to inadequate sleep, diminished neurocognitive functioning, health problems, injuries, and errors,[2] all of which can color nurses' feelings about their work and their efficacy.

Long, stressful work shifts are only exacerbated by onerous tasks unrelated to patient care. Electronic health records, advanced procedural technology, ongoing education, and training in ever-changing regulatory and accreditation requirements remove nurses from patients and, by extension, from the joy and meaning they derive from their work. In this environment, tools, technologies, and interventions designed to improve patient care and increase its safety and efficiency can't reduce nurses' stress. Best practices like rounding, bedside shift report/handoff, and leader rounding can feel like extra burdens, leading to discouragement, apathy, and frustration.

With more than half of all RNs[3] experiencing dissatisfaction, disengagement, and signs of burnout, our hospitals are at risk. In addition to an association with physical and mental health problems among nurses themselves,[4] nurse burnout has been linked to an increased risk of hospital acquired infections,[5] medical errors,[6] and poor performance on patient experience measures.[7] Disengagement and burnout are also associated with high rates of nurse turnover,[8] which can perpetuate the cycle of burnout and vulnerability among remaining staff and significantly weaken a health system's bottom line. The average turnover cost for a bedside RN is over $50,000, costing the average hospital $5.7 million based on current turnover statistics, according to the "2019 National Health Care Retention & RN Staffing Report."[9] Above and beyond turnover costs, we should consider lost reimbursement dollars tied to diminished performance on measures of safety, quality, and experience, and waning patient loyalty. Nurse disengagement puts lives at risk—a cost that we can't begin to quantify.

Improving Nurse Engagement: Thinking Strategically About Data

To overcome this crisis, we need strategies built around robust, actionable data. The sheer amount of data that healthcare leaders must review on a daily, monthly, and annual basis is staggering. Healthcare leaders often feel compelled to respond to numerous, disparate data points with immediate action plans. If sophisticated and meaningful analyses don't guide those plans (and they often don't), leaders implement a hodgepodge of interventions and short-lived improvements, struggling with performance dips as efforts shift to the next new initiative. Caregivers and leaders come away feeling that they can never quite gain enough traction to sustain meaningful improvement. Soon enough, so-called initiative fatigue sets in.

To disrupt this pattern, leaders should use clinical nursing indicators and integrated analytics to identify priority nurse engagement actions that align with the organization's goals and that impact safety, quality, and experience of care most powerfully. Clinical indicators for nursing are quantitative structure, process, and outcome measures that assess nursing-sensitive patient care and support service activities. Nurse-focused databases include Press Ganey's National Database of Nursing Quality Indicators® (NDNQI®) and its Collaborative Alliance for Nursing Outcomes (CALNOC). NDNQI measures capture nurse satisfaction, practice environment, and nursing-sensitive indicators (NSIs), while CALNOC also includes clinical indicators relevant for the acute care and ambulatory settings.

At the macro level, leaders can use cross-domain analytics to explore associations between organizational performance on these and other measures, such as safety, patient experience, and overall workforce engagement. The insights that result can guide leaders in targeting improvement efforts.

Press Ganey researchers used this approach to examine relationships between staffing measures from NDNQI; insights from RNs relative to their practice environment; and other data related to patient experience, safety, quality, the Value-Based Purchasing (VBP) Program, and readmissions. The findings showed that staffing and to an even greater extent the nurse work environment significantly impacted safety, quality, and patient experience performance. With respect to satisfaction and engagement, the nurse work environment exerted the strongest influence. Significant differences in nurses' intent to stay in their jobs and job satisfaction scores emerged between the least and most favorable work environments, leading researchers to conclude that creating a positive, healthy work environment was key to improving nurse satisfaction and engagement.[10]

Additional research examined the differences between nurse surveillance and perceptions of safety. Using the same cross-domain approach, researchers analyzed composite measures for nurses' perceptions of surveillance capacity (the presence of resources to ensure that nurses could effectively monitor and care for their patients throughout the shift) and safety.[11] Researchers found that nurses' perceptions of both were positively associated with the following three measures of nurse engagement: nurses' job satisfaction, perceptions that they were meaningfully contributing, and intent to stay (Figure 7.1). These findings suggest the importance of supplying adequate resources to support surveillance, assessing nurse perceptions of safety on an ongoing basis, and promoting and supporting nurses' emotional and physical well-being.

In a separate analysis examining the link between nurse manager ratings and patient and nurse outcomes as well as clinical nurses' perceptions of their work environment, researchers

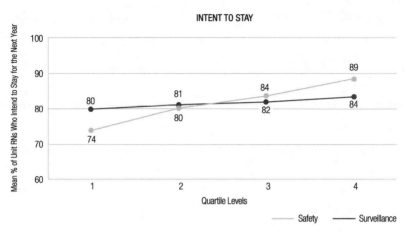

Figure 7.1   Impact of Safety and Surveillance Capacity on Nurse Intent to Stay

analyzed the impact of various aspects of the work and practice environment.[12] The findings revealed that high-performing nurse managers play a key role in creating and sustaining healthy work environments that in turn enhance clinical nurse satisfaction and engagement and lower nurse turnover across most care settings (Table 7.1). In accompanying qualitative interviews designed to identify common behaviors and practices of high-performing managers, interviewees consistently invoked an unwavering focus on providing safe, quality care. They also highlighted the importance of a culture of respect as well as nurse manager visibility, staff development, and support. As regards the latter, high-performing nurse managers leverage performance data to drive practice improvement rather than focusing on the score per se.

At Baptist Health in Lexington, Kentucky, chief nursing officer (CNO) Dr. Karen Hill understands how important the unit nurse manager role is in engaging nurse clinicians and other members of the healthcare team. Hill has advocated for a well-developed strategy and action plan to engage and support nurse managers, whom she calls the healthcare system's chief cultural officers. The action plan's essential elements include providing

Table 7.1   Impact of Nurse Managers on Work Environment

	CC	SD	MS	Rehab	ED	Amb	Periop
Autonomy	◆	◆	◆	◆	◆	◆	◆
Professional Development	◆	◆	◆	◆	◆	◆	◆
Nurse–Nurse Interaction	◆	◆	◆	◆	◆	◆	◆
Nurse–Physician Relations	◆	◆	◆	◆	◆	◆	◆
Quality Improvement	◆	◆	◆	◆	◆	◆	◆
Safe Patient Handling Mobility Protocol	◆	◆	◆	◆	◆	◆	◆
Appropriate Staffing Level	◆	◆	◆		◆	◆	◆
Unsafe Staffing Practices	◆◆	◆◆	◆◆		◆◆	◆◆	◆◆

◆ Indicates statistically meaningful relationship in positive direction

◆◆ Indicates statistically meaningful relationship in negative direction—better nurse managers engage in fewer unsafe staffing practices (i.e., safer staffing)

nurse managers with professional development opportunities, ensuring their success in their current roles and advancing their careers; working with nurse managers to develop data management and finance skills; monitoring nurse managers on an ongoing basis to ensure that they maintain the appropriate scope and span of control; supporting robust RN training; and holding clinical staff accountable, which decreases nurse manager workload and stress. This thoughtful approach leads nurse managers to seek out educational opportunities for personal growth and promotes work–life balance, both of which drive overall engagement.[13]

In a study designed to identify trends in RNs' intent to stay in their jobs, researchers found that nurses younger than 30 years old were the most likely to indicate an intent to leave their position within one year, often citing dissatisfaction with the work environment as a driving factor.[14] In the same study, job satisfaction and joy in work predicted retention most strongly in the overall sample, followed by nurse manager support, career development, and praise and recognition—all of which mattered more than influence over schedule and staffing. Differences nonetheless emerged with nurse tenure. Praise and recognition, nurse manager support, certification, and joy in work predicted intent to stay for newly licensed nurses, while CNO leadership, influence over schedule, and quality of care predicted it for nurses who had been practicing for 20 or more years. These and other age- and tenure-related differences indicate that leaders should customize engagement strategies according to the makeup of the nurse workforce.

Understanding, Addressing, and Preventing Nurse Burnout

Burnout represents the most insidious threat to nurse engagement. As described in Chapter 9, burnout is a constellation of symptoms that includes, per one specialist, "physical and emotional exhaustion," "cynicism and detachment," and "feelings of ineffectiveness and lack of accomplishment."[15] While burnout constitutes an ongoing concern across different healthcare professions, the number of nurses reporting symptoms of burnout is truly alarming. In one recent study, 63 percent of nurses in acute care settings reported symptoms of burnout.[16] Given this prevalence and the evidence linking nurse burnout and the quality of patient care,[17] burnout represents nothing less than a public health crisis.

To address this problem, healthcare leaders must first understand its risks, protective factors, and the relative balance of such factors across nurse segments. Healthcare-provider burnout is largely a function of two overarching considerations: the degree to which caregivers find their work motivating and meaningful (activation) and the degree to which they can disconnect from work and recharge (decompression). Internal and external sources of stress and rewards on the job influence activation and decompression, and the relative influence of all these variables hinges on resilience.[18]

Research suggests that individuals' resilience to burnout depends on where they fall on the activation and decompression spectrum, which we can measure using a validated tool comprising a subset of engagement survey questions.[19] As with nurse engagement in general, nurse resilience can vary widely by generation, tenure, and role.[20] For both nurse managers and bedside nurses, job enjoyment relates strongly to activation. For managers, it also relates to safety and a sense of pride in their quality of service, while for nonmanagers, taking personal pride in their work leads to job enjoyment. Among both managers and nonmanagers, the ability to decompress is related to nurses' own perceptions of their stress and their organizations' support of work–life balance.

Other differences exist across cohorts. Managers' perceptions of their own stress are linked to resource availability and staffing considerations. For nonmanagers, perceived stress stems from feeling heard, securing strong feedback, and being assigned clear tasks. Across generations, work enjoyment and nurses' perceptions of stress drive resilience. For baby boomers, resilience hinges on the availability of resources and an ability to take pride in the quality of care. For Generation X, resilience has more to do with perceptions of organizational safety, diversity, and community, and a sense of being heard by managers and the organization. Resilience among millennial and Generation Y nurses relates most to clarity about roles and responsibilities and the perception that managers and the organization respect them.[21] Understanding all of these differences is essential for developing targeted solutions.

As an illustration, consider Greenville, North Carolina–based Vidant Health's efforts to enhance nurse engagement and retention. Upon studying its annual engagement insights, Vidant identified the lowest levels of engagement among nurses younger than 25 years of age. To understand this trend more deeply, Vidant coupled exit interview findings from nurses in this age group with qualitative analysis from their engagement survey. As Vidant found, younger nurses were leaving out of concern for their schedule, hours, and work–life balance. Leaders heard story after story of nurses who sought to balance work with family responsibilities, who struggled to work overtime, 12-hour, and rotating shifts, and who found it hard to take time off for family needs. As a result, nurses were having a harder time coping with stress. Many were choosing to leave the organization.

Vidant Health revamped how it scheduled and hired new nurses, abandoning the "12-hour-only" shift model. Leaders developed a robust "stay interview" process, capturing more real-time feedback from employed nurses on issues that would potentially incline them to leave in the next year. Such interviews allowed Vidant to address such issues proactively, before it was too late. To assess this work's effectiveness, Vidant Health added an item to their engagement survey querying whether nurses had a one-on-one "stay interview" with their leader. Julie Kennedy Oehlert, DNP, RN, chief experience officer for Vidant Health, noted, "We know that the key to nurse engagement will come from the voice of our nurses, and that when we improve our engagement, all other outcomes will follow!"[22]

Caring for Our Nurse Caregivers

To design a successful strategy for improving nurse engagement, leaders must understand the totality of the nurse experience. Start by understanding patient needs, since these influence the caregiver experience. The Compassionate Connected Care™ model, based on a qualitative survey of caregivers and developed to help reduce patient suffering, is composed of themes in four categories: connectedness, clinical excellence, operational excellence, and culture.[23] Because the relative importance of each of these categories may vary by caregiver type, care setting, department, or unit, leaders should assess engagement data in depth to gauge how well their organization is meeting patient needs and to design improvement plans targeting specific subpopulations. To this end, leaders can use the strategies for data gathering, goal setting, and change management described earlier in the book. Leaders can customize these strategies by asking questions about the definition of nursing excellence, the organization's position on the journey, and the infrastructure that exists to enable, measure, and report on engagement.

In the early stages of planning, leaders should identify key stakeholders and partners. The first question to consider: "Who owns nurse engagement?" While the answer should be self-evident (nurse engagement is a shared responsibility), unit-level nurse managers can often feel that they bear sole responsibility for nurse engagement.

Nurse leaders should adopt a broader perspective and identify who in the organization is best positioned to influence nurse engagement. As indicated earlier, nurse engagement derives from a positive work environment, and stakeholders include senior and mid-level nurse leaders, clinical staff, physicians, and other clinical professionals. Looking beyond nursing, senior administrative leaders such as the chief operating officer and chief financial officer strongly influence nurse engagement, as they decide how to allocate financial and other resources.

To improve engagement, leaders should enlist subject matter experts with deep understanding of and experience with engagement, recruitment, and retention. Leaders should also build a solid partnership between nursing and HR by sharing expertise; aligning around nurse engagement, recruitment, and retention; and establishing accountability. Establishing clear ownership and accountability among stakeholders was a game changer for one large academic medical center on the West Coast. Nursing and HR leaders worked together to develop goals around RN engagement, recruitment, and retention. They instituted nursing retention councils, enhanced interdisciplinary rounds and partnerships, developed a workplace violence steering group, and increased their focus on caregiver retention. Over a two-year period, the health system achieved significant gains in RN engagement scores and an estimated return on investment of $3.2 million through increased revenue, cost avoidance, and cost reduction.

The outcomes of unit- and department-level gap assessments should inform goal setting for enhanced nurse engagement, while a focused and detailed operational plan should determine execution. Internal initiatives, such as those described earlier, and external programs can help frame the engagement journey and key milestones. External programs include the American Nurses

Credentialing Center Magnet Recognition Program®, its Pathway to Excellence Program®, and the American Association of Critical-Care Nurses Beacon Award for Excellence. All of these programs use evidence-based standards informed by a substantial body of research into healthy and positive work environments. In addition, nurse work environments boasting high retention rates can yield valuable lessons. Qualitative findings from units in which all clinical staff responded that they intend to stay on their unit have revealed helpful tactics, including recruiting nurses who take joy in their work, providing support to nurses, and ensuring the right staff tenure mix, as illustrated in Table 7.2.

Table 7.2 Nurse Engagement Practices from High-Intent-to-Stay Units

Engagement Themes	Retention Tactics
Quality of Care/Joy in Work	• Recruit and hire nurses who share organizational values. • Model and expect an unwavering focus on quality of care. • Create an environment that optimizes the rewards of nursing and minimizes the influence of associated stressors.
Manager Support	• Support staff nurses' professional and career development goals. • Encourage open communication and provide regular guidance and feedback. • Cultivate a team of high-performing nurse managers to provide the support and leadership that new and experienced nurses need to be satisfied and successful.
Staff Tenure Mix	• Ensure an appropriate mix of tenured and newly licensed RNs. • Hire to the right skill set. • Recruit experienced staff who are interested and invested in mentoring newer nurses.
Workforce Cohesion	• Foster a positive culture of teamwork and support in which newly licensed RNs are welcomed and nurtured. • Encourage and recognize participation by RNs at all levels on the unit in the process of building and growing this culture.
Staffing and Scheduling	• Commit to staffing levels that protect patient and nurse safety. • Staff units based on patient acuity. • Offer self-scheduling and flexible schedule options to optimize work–life balance and job satisfaction.

Toward a Workforce of Engaged Nurses

When healthcare organizations develop a thoughtful strategy, align leaders and stakeholders around goals, focus their efforts, and execute with precision, nurse engagement increases and overall outcomes improve. That was the case for a large rehabilitation hospital in the Midwest, which fully revamped its nurse recruiting, onboarding, and retention strategies to help its new and established nurses find joy in their work and deliver a better patient experience. Despite having to hire nurses at an unusually high rate to accommodate a new unit's staffing needs, hospital leadership developed a plan that prioritized the fit of employees to organizational culture rather than how quickly the hospital filled vacant positions. To assess fit, leaders required that every applicant submit a behavior-based assessment, created a structured interviewing guide and peer-interviewing teams, and implemented mandatory job shadowing.

As new nurses signed on, leaders began to focus on retention efforts, including the initiation of a 60-day new-hire lunch, the distribution of "total compensation statements" to clarify the breadth of benefits nurses received, and regular recognition for nurses who went above the call of duty to improve the patient experience of care. Since implementing the changes in 2016, the hospital's patient experience and RN engagement rankings rose to the 99th percentile, and nurse turnover decreased more than 10 percent, potentially saving millions of dollars per year in recruitment and training costs.

When health system leaders help nurses and other team members find joy and meaning in their work, the benefits are immense. Nurses become happier, healthier, and more resilient, and they want to stay in their jobs longer. In turn, the teams they work with and the patients they serve become happier and healthier, as does the organization. As elusive as it currently is, nurse engagement is well worth pursuing—for everyone's sake.

IN SUM

- Nurse engagement contributes to excellence in healthcare, affecting the safety, quality, and experience of patient care.
- Using nursing clinical indicators and integrated analytics, health systems should identify nurse engagement actions that will maximally impact safety, quality, and experience of care.
- There is no one-size-fits-all engagement strategy to meet nurses' needs. Leaders must instead frame strategies to address the varying needs of nurses across age, tenure, and role.
- Nurse leaders should seek to understand the shared and varying drivers of activation and decompression in different nurse segments to determine which teams are vulnerable to burnout. Leaders should also adopt organizational strategies and best practices for bolstering nurse resilience.

CHAPTER

8

Bolstering Physician Engagement and Resilience

Chrissy Daniels, MS, and Matt Turner, MA

> *Unless healthcare systems help physicians become more engaged and resilient on the job, safe, high-quality care for patients and communities will remain elusive. In an age of escalating physician shortages and rising consumerism in healthcare, leading organizations treat physician engagement as a competitive advantage, redesigning their cultures to bolster physician engagement and resilience.*

IT'S NOT EASY being a doctor in America today. Dr. Anne Pendo, the senior medical director for physician engagement at Intermountain Healthcare, is a highly engaged leader within the health system, as well as a mentor, a mother, and a physician resilience champion. And yet, as she told us, she struggled with burnout brought on by excessive bureaucratic procedures.[1] Pendo recounted having to spend nights and weekends auditing charts, as mandated by the Centers for Medicare & Medicaid Services (CMS), so that they would be ready by the end of the calendar year. "When New Year's Eve finally arrived," she told us, "I drove to the post office in the snow to get my audits postmarked by that date and discovered it was closed.

As I knocked on the door, begging for somebody to come help me, tears streaming down my face, I thought, 'Has my life really come to this? Can I really continue doing this work next year? Will this be my job and life until I retire?'"

As Pendo reflected, the need to perform so much administrative work caused her to lose the "ability to continue to connect with my patients in a meaningful way while still parenting my three little kids. I wasn't about to sacrifice parenting for data entry. So, shortly after the post office incident, I realized, *I can't sustain this.* I knew instinctively that I couldn't be the only one who felt this way."

Sadly, she isn't. Physician engagement has been declining for over a decade. The number of doctors who report "liking the work" is in freefall, physician burnout has reached epidemic levels,[2] and 22 percent of final-year medical students wish they had selected a different career.[3] The culprits are many and include rising daily demands on physicians, pressures on doctors created by heightened public transparency, ICD-10 (*International Statistical Classification of Diseases and Related Health Problems,* 10th Revision) documentation, the Medicare Access and CHIP Reauthorization Act of 2015, and the rise of site-specific care segmentation (i.e., hospitalists). Although doctors tend to rank time with patients as among the most rewarding aspects of their jobs,[4] in the interests of greater efficiency and more "accountability" clinicians are dedicating more of their time to staring at a computer screen. In effect, the cherished American ideal of productivity is clashing with fundamental clinical care values like patient-centricity. The healthcare industry in general, and physicians in particular, are pushing hard for both values at once—with alarming results. A recent study conservatively pegged burnout's economic damage each year at $4.6 billion, taking into account costs associated with turnover and reduced clinical hours.[5]

Survey data afford us a more precise picture of why physicians become disillusioned. The 2019 Medscape survey results, which largely replicate the 2018 findings, find that 59 percent of over 15,000 respondents perceive "too many bureaucratic tasks" as a top source of stress, followed by "spending too many hours at work" (34 percent), the electronic health record (EHR) (32 percent), lack of respect from colleagues and administrators (30 percent), and "insufficient compensation" (29 percent).[6] Press Ganey's research confirms these findings. We've pioneered a model of physician resilience and engagement (Chapter 9) that underscores the importance that stressors and rewards play in either enhancing or inhibiting physician engagement. According to the more than 94,000 physicians that Press Ganey surveys each year, "I get the tools and resources I need to provide the best care and service for patients" is one of the top drivers of physician engagement.[7] Sadly, this is also one of the lowest scoring items within the physician database, and physicians rate this item significantly lower than all other healthcare workers. Whether they are affiliated with a hospital or health system or work for a clinic, physicians struggle, in part, because they lack the support needed to thrive in practice.

Disenchantment with workplace conditions leads many doctors to limit their practice or leave the profession before their full retirement age, and it also encourages many potential students to bypass a career in medicine. The result is a shortage of doctors, one that the Association of American Medical Colleges (AAMC) projects will only worsen over time. While in 2019 the industry was short nearly 30,000 highly trained and expert clinicians, this number will conservatively swell to anywhere from 46,900 to 121,300 by 2032.[8] The shortfall will impact primary and specialty care, including mental health, in roughly equal measure even when accounting for a range of countervailing developments, such as the expected growth in the supply of advanced practitioners, the postponement of retirement by retirement-age physicians, and changes in reimbursement models.

Healthcare organizations understand that many doctors feel besieged and unhappy in their jobs. But well-intentioned improvement efforts remain either overly tactical or extremely conceptual, often neglecting core issues. In many instances, such efforts waste both physicians' scarcest resource—time—as well as organizational resources. We can and must do better.

When it comes to safety, the Institute of Medicine's *To Err Is Human: Building a Safer Health System* (1999)[9] inspired many hospitals and clinicians to reconsider the efficacy of their care processes. The report instigated a national "soul-searching" that eventually crystallized into the objective of achieving Zero Harm. Organizations then began defining the problem, setting goals, and allocating resources to achieve their aim. After 20 years of progress, work remains ongoing. We need a similar national awakening to address declining physician engagement and rising burnout. Given the impending shortages in physician supply, organizations can't wait for 20 years to take meaningful action. Physician engagement is a business and moral imperative, intimately linked to clinical quality, profitability, and a range of other objectives, including physicians' own personal and professional fulfillment. Healthcare's overarching goal is to ameliorate suffering, heal patients when possible, and help patients adjust and achieve quality of life when their afflictions exceed the capabilities of modern medicine. We should want nothing less for the clinicians providing the care.

Organizing to Improve

Some organizations have gone further than most in addressing physician disengagement and burnout, with impressive results. These organizations have taken the important first steps of identifying burnout as a problem, prioritizing physician engagement, and analyzing root causes. They've accepted that the organization bears a shared responsibility with individual physicians for advancing the work. They've also partnered with physicians to redefine the very nature of collaboration within their culture and the broader physician community. They've redesigned organizational systems for communication, governance, and decision-making to foster greater physician resilience and fulfillment and ensure that changes are sustainable over time.

As these organizations know, physician engagement starts at the top. Chief executive officers (CEOs) must commit sufficient prioritization, resources, and accountability to advance the organization. Kevin Manemann, executive vice president and chief executive for Providence St. Joseph Health's physician enterprise, has elevated physician engagement to a top strategic priority. His organization devotes time, attention, and resources to engagement improvements and continues to redefine and improve how physicians and administrators interact. Every year, Providence St. Joseph measures physician engagement as a first step to marking its progress. Based on physician feedback, the leaders responsible for the entire enterprise of 6,000-plus employed physicians select "the one big thing" to address that year. Each region, service line, and individual clinic must also craft an appropriate "local" plan. The executive team meets quarterly to review all plans, assessing progress, understanding barriers, and celebrating wins. The goal is to create a cycle of continuous improvement, ongoing organizational dialogue, and adaptability.

Once leading-edge organizations mobilize to reduce physician burnout and promote engagement as a strategic priority, as Providence St. Joseph Health has done, they invest in the teams and resources needed to tackle the problem. This often begins with nomination of a physician leader to develop the strategy and partner with operational and support leaders to execute it. Physician leaders can come from varied backgrounds, but prerequisites for the job include a strong personal vision for the work, a demonstrated ability to work collaboratively and cooperatively across departments, and the ability to persevere in the face of complex problems.

Dr. Paul Cullen, vice president of medical affairs at Washington Health System, is one such physician leader. Serving several communities in rural southwestern Pennsylvania, his organization faces aggressive competition from a variety of larger players. Cullen and CEO Gary Weinstein have led the charge to redesign their organization to support a thriving medical community, and especially to achieve high engagement by fostering cooperation and collaboration across multiple stakeholder groups. "Getting the whole team to think about the problem was the key to addressing it," says Cullen.

Cullen ensures that reviewing the annual physician engagement results is not simply a one-and-done conversation. Dr. John Six and Brook Ward, recent successors to Cullen and Weinstein, continue to believe that a multidimensional approach is key to driving caregiver engagement. The executive team holds frequent conversations about physician engagement, and so does the medical executive committee and the organization's all-physician meetings. Ward and Six routinely schedule outreach meetings with physician groups in their community to discuss engagement.

Beyond individual leadership, organizations need project management and administrative support. To obtain it, they must build a coalition of leaders throughout the organization with expertise in areas such as leadership development, project management, internal communications, information technology, EHR optimization, and nursing and operational leadership. Physician engagement is a *systemic* problem and as such requires resources spanning all parts of the system. After the all-important decision to prioritize physician engagement, perhaps the most important contribution system leaders can make is to mobilize and align the necessary resources.

In addition, executives must support a seamless transition from strategic plan to improvement priorities, documenting specific improvements as they occur. To support this level of accountability, the CEO should commit the organization to regularly measuring physician engagement. Traditionally, many organizations have either failed to measure physician engagement, or they did so infrequently (once every three to five years). Leaders at high-performing organizations realize the importance of annual measurement using culture surveys, along with six-month and episodic pulse surveys.

The Importance of Shared Purpose

Even with passionate leaders who prioritize physician engagement, build an aligned operational coalition, and measure effectively, improvement efforts can fail. Individual doctors must also buy in and contribute. In most professions, employees commit to improvement initiatives based on self-interest alone, but that's not enough in medicine. To truly activate physicians, organizations must convince them that they are not only dedicated to their fulfillment at work, but equally important, to patient safety and care. That's because the practice of medicine usually begins with a robust connection to purpose. Many practicing physicians first pursued medicine for altruistic or social reasons, embracing medicine as their calling early—often in early adolescence. For them, engagement hinges on a deeply felt sense that they are helping patients become healthier and making a difference in their lives.

As organizations compete more feverishly to attract doctors, those that deliver safe, high-quality, patient-centered care *and* treat physicians well will win the talent race. A national analysis of 2018 physician engagement data reveals a strong relationship between physicians' perception of care quality at their organization and their likelihood to recommend the organization to family and friends (Figure 8.1). When physicians believe the organization shares their values and is dedicated to delivering the best care to patients, both organizational engagement and physician retention also increase.

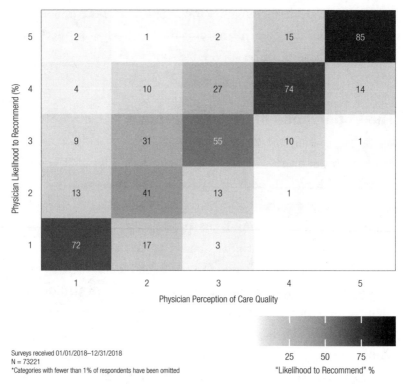

Figure 8.1. Proportion of Physician Likelihood to Recommend a Hospital by Physician Perception of Care Quality

Source: "A Unified Approach to Drive Patient and Physician Loyalty," Press Ganey, June 6, 2019, 4.

To attract and retain physicians, organizations must commit to patient care by declaring Zero Harm as an organizational goal (see Chapter 11) and elevating patient experience to a strategic priority. Acting on these two key steps requires action at the system, local, and individual levels. Physicians must share an organization's purpose and perceive that the organization is implementing evidence-based behaviors that result in better and safer patient care. Physicians must also become involved in strategy development and daily operations, perceiving that the organization is taking their perspectives seriously.

One organization that has taken concrete action here is Intermountain Healthcare. Leaders there have implemented a daily huddle process across 24 hospitals (including one virtual hospital) and 160 clinics. The process mandates a series of 15-minute huddles, starting with frontline caregivers, progressing to directors, hospital leadership, and regional senior leaders, and concluding with the CEO and his direct reports. The huddle covers a predetermined agenda, beginning with serious safety events or near misses and any caregiver safety concerns, and followed by important operational themes. The goal is to identify obstacles in real time and put responses in place, with leaders doing so in a timely and transparent manner. Daily huddles have allowed the organization to become far more agile and responsive in identifying concerns and enacting safety solutions.[10]

The 10 physician engagement survey items that most predict physician commitment illustrate the close connection between engagement and action taken on behalf of patients and their care. These items are "This organization provides high-quality care and service," "This clinic/group makes every effort to deliver safe, error-free care to patients," "Overall, I believe my patients feel highly satisfied with the care they receive," "My work unit works well together," "This clinic/group cares about quality improvement," "There is effective teamwork between physicians and nurses," "I get the tools and resources I need to provide the best care for patients," "I have adequate input into decisions that affect how I practice medicine," "Administration is responsive to feedback from physicians/providers," and "There is a climate of trust in this organization." Significantly, 3 of these top 10 drivers identify in explicit language the organization's commitment to providing quality care, as well as the physician's own belief in the consistency of that commitment.

Moving Toward High Reliability

Let's take a closer look at these survey items. The first three—"This organization provides high-quality care and service," "This clinic/group makes every effort to deliver safe, error-free care to patients," and "Overall, I believe my patients feel highly satisfied with the care they receive"—speak to physician impressions of the *reliability* with which the organization delivers safe, high-quality, patient-centered care. When High Reliability, safety, and experience are in place, engagement increases and more physicians agree with the statement, "My patients are not harmed and have great outcomes, and I have meaningful professional connections with my patients and teams." The potential for decompression increases as well, with more physicians agreeing with survey items that represent sentiments like, "I am able to trust the care that nursing delivers," "I do not have to race to provide personal solutions to systemic problems," and "I can relax when I'm away from the organization because there are processes and teams in place to ensure the reliable delivery of care."

Although simple in concept, reliable delivery of excellent patient care is complex to execute. Highly reliable organizations embrace principles of process design, reliability culture, and human factors integration. Process design requires that organizations embrace evidence-based best practices, reviewing key clinical care processes as well as focusing and simplifying processes and procedures. For example, identify the key processes that deliver optimal outcomes and bundle them to increase the compliance with which they are completed.

Cultural norms are also key, especially insofar as they make possible a sense of psychological safety within an organization. Highly reliable organizations sustain improvements by making explicit the core values that should inform decision-making across the organization. In addition to stated values, the organization must define required behaviors, setting clear expectations for everyone. Leaders must also protect and reinforce these norms by coaching others and implementing accountability procedures. Dr. Virginia Casey, chief medical officer of OrthoCarolina, a large independent orthopedic group serving the Carolinas, has created a formalized mentor program to help build relationships and normalize practices such as operating together, providing peer-to-peer coaching, and relaying the group's values and performance expectations. While the mentoring program lasts three years for any new physician, it serves as a springboard to informal mentoring over the course of a career.[11] Casey calls the program "a grassroots strategy" and credits it as "pivotal to her efforts to facilitate meaningful culture change—one physician at a time."[12]

With both process and cultural improvements underway, the organization should continue to refine performance by designing safety into the system. It's not enough to rely on an individual physician's commitment to excellence. Despite the commitment and resilience of healthcare's workforce, the industry itself is so complex that even the most vigilant individuals can't ensure the delivery of safe care. Organizations must follow the lead of industries such as nuclear power and aeronautics and embrace a discipline known as human factors design, which creates structural barriers preventing individuals from making mistakes and helps them discharge tasks properly each and every time. As we explore in Chapter 10, High Reliability cultures ensure that more patients receive the best possible care and that teams and individuals are better coordinated and psychologically safe. This, in turn, creates deeper levels of engagement for all caregivers.

Leading Change in Practice

Another four survey items on the previous list—"My work unit works well together," "This clinic/group cares about quality improvement," "There is effective teamwork between physicians and nurses," and "I receive the tools and resources I need to provide the best care for patients"—speak to how important it is that physicians feel empowered to act on patients' behalf. Despite their status as key internal stakeholders in any healthcare organization, physicians across the country report feeling less power to influence their daily work than other healthcare employees do.[13] As performance measurement increasingly creeps into medical practice, as organizations demand increased productivity, and as patient expectations swell, the autonomy accorded to physicians shrinks. Whereas the practice of medicine was once largely individual and independent, physicians must now serve as team leaders, process designers, and organizational influencers if they are to influence patient care. Sadly, medical school curricula and residency training don't impart such skills. Training doctors in continuous improvement and leadership skills increases their sense of their own power, leading to better organizational performance. Armed with these skills, physicians can empower their colleagues and teams to solve problems for their patients and practice, thus creating new efficiencies in the physician's practice.

One training program that has helped restore a sense of autonomy to doctors is Salem Health's Physician Leadership Institute (PLI). Pioneered nearly a decade ago, PLI comprises cohort-based learning sessions and applied improvement projects. PLI participants learn team-based approaches to problem-solving, and master foundational quality improvement, project management, change management, and leadership principles. Training sessions allow learners to experience work as part of a dyad with an administrative leader partner, and to develop new levels of connection, trust, and collegiality within the cohort.[14]

Supporting Individual Physicians

A final set of survey items from the preceding list—"I have adequate input into decisions that affect how I practice medicine," "Administration is responsive to feedback from physicians/providers," and "There is a climate of trust in this organization"—relate to how well physicians feel their organizations listen and respond to their concerns. Physicians want to feel supported and influence the decision-making process, but they often feel that leaders don't welcome their input. Clearly, organizations must provide physicians with the ability to provide input, but engagement among physicians hinges on whether they perceive that the organization truly *listens* to them and addresses their concerns. Unfortunately, physicians consistently rate their organizations' performance in this area among the lowest of all items in the Press Ganey physician database. Physicians also rate these items significantly lower than other healthcare workers do.

It's so important for organizations to listen, because any burnout reduction strategy must consider the heavy burdens that individual physicians bear. Physicians aren't vehicles for increasing access or generating cases. Their work–life balance matters. Leading organizations recognize this and lend them support through professional mentoring and confidential employee assistance programs. But they go further. Rather than waiting for an individual physician to seek help, leading organizations provide physicians with mentoring and skills development so that doctors can integrate their professional and personal lives more effectively. These organizations actively cultivate peer connections and camaraderie among physicians, creating safe places in which doctors can discuss the joys and stresses of their jobs and fight the lone-liness so prevalent among physicians today. Whether through breakfast clubs, informal book clubs, dinner meetings, or other similar mechanisms, leading organizations create spaces for physi-cians to come together in the community for support, recognition, and learning.

Novant Health is one such organization. With the sponsor-ship of CEO Carl Amato and under the leadership of Dr. Tom E. Jenike, senior vice president and chief human experience officer, Novant has spearheaded a systematic effort to address physician burnout.[15] The intervention begins by taking physicians off-site for a course focusing on resilience and leadership, and is reinforced with mentoring, coaching, personal reflection, mindfulness, and other leadership development techniques. The goal is to help phy-sicians effectively lead, cultivate meaningful patient and colleague relationships, and maintain a healthy personal life. As a result of this extensive program, in 2018 Novant ranked in the 90th per-centile for physician engagement in the Press Ganey National Database.

Salem Health worked with an outside expert to create its Team Resiliency Institute (TRI), composed initially of 100 offi-cial and unofficial Salem Health leaders. TRI cohorts learn evidence-based resilience tools that they apply in team settings with guidance from Salem Health leadership. Salem Health's chief medical officer, Ralph Yates, describes the course's focus as "enhancing system-wide resiliency, recognizing that burn-out affects physicians, nurses, and staff alike."[16] As Yates further reflects, the greatest benefit of such skill-building efforts has been in the boost it has given to the organization's culture. "We have come to understand that professional isolation, loneliness, is driv-ing burnout. Establishment of collegial teams helps combat this through the development of enhanced resiliency." Organizations like Salem Health have moved beyond simply talking about work–life balance, providing organizational support and skill-building that arm physicians with the tools necessary to integrate work and home life.

To further support individual physicians, organizations should maintain transparent channels of communication. Physicians must understand how, where, and when decisions are made, and have regular opportunities to influence decisions that impact their practice. Most healthcare organizations have trouble effectively incorporating physicians' input into organizational decisions. And yet, as noted in Chapter 1, three significant megatrends related to technology, demographics, and care delivery pose significant risks for many healthcare organizations. All three also acutely impact physicians. Whether through formal appointments and creating a dyadic (administrator–physician) leadership structure, through less formal but permanent augmented committee structures, or through a redefined role for the medical executive committee, or all of the above, leading organizations bring physicians more fully into the problem-solving process.

The Future

Healthcare organizations can and must do more to address the problem of declining physician engagement and rising levels of burnout. Leaders must go beyond their familiar, piecemeal tactics and devise broader, transformational solutions to burnout. They must bring vitality back to the practice of medicine—not just for the doctors' sake, but for the patients' sake. When she reflects on the problem of physician engagement, Intermountain Healthcare's Dr. Pendo always returns to patients, because caring for them is what most physicians ultimately care about. "I want to hear physicians and APPs talk about their personal connection to our organization's purpose and to our patients," she says.

"I want to hear about, 'Oh, I had this great conversation with my patient about . . . ,' instead of, 'When will we fix the EHR.' I want our physicians to feel connected to their patients, to each other, to their leaders, and the organization. I want to transform healthcare." It's a noble goal and one that should capture the imagination of healthcare leaders everywhere.

IN SUM

- Physician burnout constitutes one of the most pressing challenges in healthcare today, with the potential to cause a severe shortage of physicians.
- Leaders must measure physician burnout, resilience, and engagement with their practices, teams, and organizations.
- Organizations must empower physician leaders to develop a comprehensive improvement strategy, aligning stakeholders across the organization to provide institutional support.
- Organizations should commit to the delivery of safe, high-quality, patient-centered care, since most physicians feel deeply committed to providing it.
- Organizations should empower physicians by providing them with continuous improvement and leadership skills, employee assistance, peer mentoring, and work–life integration support.

CHAPTER
9

Contextualizing Resilience

Deirdre E. Mylod, PhD, and
Thomas H. Lee, MD, MSc

The cultivation of resilience is critical to warding off burnout, as it allows employees to learn from setbacks and remain flexible in fraught situations. But when organizations unduly emphasize resilience, they sometimes "blame the victim" and overlook their own role in helping avoid burnout. Organizations need a framework for better identifying burnout's causes, their own role in preventing it, and resilience's role in sustaining engagement and promoting wellness.

OVER THE PAST half century, technological advances have broadly transformed healthcare. Previously untreatable diseases have become curable, and conditions that once led to rapid decline and death have become chronic and manageable. But as wonderful as this change has been, it has also placed quite a strain on healthcare providers. There's now so much more to do when delivering care and so much more information to manage. At the same time, it has become easier than ever to make mistakes. Confronted by these pressures, clinicians and personnel have felt increasingly stressed and burned out. The problem has become so pervasive that concern about burnout has spread beyond doctors and nurses to the public at large. The World Health Organization has even formally defined burnout as an occupational phenomenon.[1]

Leaders at healthcare organizations have responded by cultivating more resilience in the workforce, boosting employees' ability to "bounce back" from challenges as they arise. Mindful that safe, high-quality, and compassionate patient care requires a healthy and engaged workforce, they've held town hall meetings in which they've expressed genuine concern about workplace stress and emphasized resilience's importance. They've also used these meetings to introduce employees to new wellness offerings, such as on-campus yoga classes, nutritional counseling, mindfulness retreats, and guided gratitude practice. Further, they've delivered the message that employees should take care of themselves by eating right and exercising, and that they should make use of their organization's system-wide employee assistance programming.

All too often, such responses have fallen flat, befuddling leaders. "When do they expect me to exercise," some clinicians think, "during early morning meetings or at night when I'm catching up with all my overdue tasks in the EHR?" Other clinicians wonder if they're supposed to come in on a Saturday to learn how to keep a journal detailing how "grateful" they are that their colleagues talk down to them in front of patients. "I'm already mindful," still others think, "I'm mindful that I just spent an hour in this meeting, which means that I'll have to stay late to get the rest of my work done and will miss my daughter's basketball game again." Perhaps most troubling are reactions that incorporate an element of self-blame. Some clinicians fault themselves for not doing more to stay healthy. They feel like they're the only ones who feel overextended and that something must be wrong with them.

In essence, leaders run astray when they frame resilience as an individual problem as opposed to an organizational one. Even when organizations approach resilience systemically, staff-level workers perceive that resilience hinges on them personally and their own ability, capacity, or willingness to cope with the environment. If they lack resilience, they must be weak or unwilling to build it. Leaders also tend to treat stress as a single, monolithic category, failing to distinguish between sources of stress that might be more emotionally intense, such as a patient death, versus small but cumulative frustrations and pressures, such as inefficient technology. As a result, remedies can feel artificial, poorly matched with individual stresses, and even ridiculous. Intense group therapy or a discussion of feelings seems unhelpful, for example, when one feels mired in hours of mind-numbing, bureaucratic tasks. Yoga classes, however therapeutic, can likewise seem trivial to someone coping with the death of a patient. As one furious physician said to one of us after getting an invitation to a "chair yoga" session: "I don't want a [expletive] yoga mat. I want three more minutes with every patient so I can feel like I am doing a good job."

Healthcare leaders need to change how they think about and respond to burnout. At present, they conceive of burnout as the emotional exhaustion and depersonalization that results from prolonged exposure to an environment of stress[2] and associate resilience with those who *don't* experience burnout.[3] They frame burnout and resilience as opposites, perceiving resilience as burnout's logical remedy. In fact, these two concepts aren't opposites, but simply alternative responses to prolonged exposure to workplace stress. Addressing burnout requires prevention, while focusing on resilience amounts to a rescue strategy once burnout has already developed. To solve the problem of burnout, leaders must focus squarely on prevention, emphasizing positive factors like engagement, wellness, and even joy.[4] They must create healthy environments where individuals can find meaning and take pride in their daily work.

Deconstructing Burnout

Before we can develop workable solutions to burnout, let's first detail the factors that produce it, and conversely, that lead to strong employee engagement. Leaders at Mayo Clinic have identified nine key topics or "leverage points" that, when dysfunctional, can lead to burnout. These include workload and job demands, a lack of meaning in work, poorly articulated organizational culture and values, and deficiencies in social support and the workplace community.[5] Unfortunately, these categories don't distinguish among the varied experiences that people have at work. The category of workload and job demands, for instance, includes topics like complexity, intensity, and high-stakes decisions that are *inherent* to patient care, regardless of where one works. But that same category also covers issues like the lack of sufficient staff to discharge responsibilities, or the lack of sufficient time to deliver safe, high-quality care. Distinguishing among sources of stress is critical to developing correct solutions. It will also make communication about burnout more effective, demonstrating to staff that you really do understand the causes of their distress.

In discussing burnout, many leaders invoke the term *work–life balance.* Beyond our general need to balance our personal and professional lives, we must strike a balance between the fulfillment work brings us and the stress it inevitably causes. Some research suggests that clinicians need at least 20 percent of their work to have meaning in order to prevent burnout.[6] In addition to the cumulative reward and stress we experience, we must also consider the *kinds* of rewards we receive and stresses we endure. Knowing you've positively impacted a patient's life or experiencing pride in your accomplishments feels fundamentally different than, say, an incentive payment or new retirement benefit. Conversely, delivering devastating news to a family about a prognosis and witnessing their anguish requires a different kind of coping strategy than wrangling with inefficient technology or managing toxic workforce relationships.

After conversing with clinicians and healthcare professionals and leaders, we created a conceptual model that organizes these rewards and stresses according to the nature of the work, and that points to the types of activities necessary to optimize fulfillment.[7] Our model distinguishes between causes or inputs that are inherent to patient care, and those that arise from the local, organizational, or industry context. An external environment that tips the balance for an individual in favor of the rewards accruing to a job promotes engagement, while stressful and burdensome environments create a greater potential for burnout and emotional exhaustion. This model illustrates the role that work settings can play in staff members' emotional lives, allowing for outcomes that are sometimes counterintuitive. A person might remain highly engaged and committed to their work even as the environment nudges them closer to burnout. Although previous models have regarded the stress involved in caregiving as a single, undifferentiated mass, something to be withstood or rejected, our model suggests how to overcome the myriad sources of clinical stress and distress in a more nuanced fashion.

Healthcare's Inherent Rewards and Stressors

Our framework conceives of patient care as an inherently good, rewarding, and meaningful activity. The rewards accruing from patient care stem from the act of providing care, rather than from the location in which you work, the era in which you practice(d), your specialty, or the local or regulatory policies that shape care delivery. Healthcare providers often speak of caring for patients as a privilege and an honor, recognizing that patients are allowing them to share their most intimate and even sacred moments. Many caregivers describe the amazing feeling of solidarity that arises among colleagues who collaborate to heal a patient. Clinicians and staff perceive how important their roles and knowledge are upon seeing patients suffer less, recover from illnesses, and return to health. Quite deservedly, they experience pride, appreciation, and even a sense of their own heroic potential. In situations when medicine can't produce a cure, clinicians and caregivers still find meaning in embarking on healing journeys with patients and offering comfort and support.

Clinicians often describe such inherent rewards as the reasons they chose to pursue medicine or healthcare, ranking them as among the best parts of their job. Such rewards are not limited to clinicians or those who directly interact with patients. Those indirectly involved in patient care also connect with healthcare's mission and consider their roles inherently important and meaningful.

As rewarding as it is, however, patient care is also inherently stressful. No matter your environment or occupational niche, providing care entails witnessing the suffering of others, delivering hard news, and bearing responsibility for high-stakes decisions. Patients don't always improve, even with the best of care. Clinicians cope with death more frequently than members of other professions do. And given healthcare's complex and fast-paced nature, caregivers must always be at their best. There is little room for error, and staff must shoulder the knowledge that a single false step could have terrible, even deadly consequences.

To understand the extent to which inherent stressors and rewards are intertwined, consider the experience that clinicians have during humanitarian aid trips. As a physician colleague told us, she had recently returned from a mission trip to Haiti, where she witnessed an incredible amount of suffering and need. Patients had traveled miles and waited in line for hours to receive care for previously untreated conditions. The work itself was exhausting, with these visiting healthcare providers working from dawn to dusk.

At the same time, the trip was an unforgettable, life-changing experience for this physician. "I never touched a computer," she said, "never touched a form or thought about insurance. All we did was care for patients. It was rejuvenating and brought me back to my mission of interacting with patients and offering personalized cures and comfort. I paid for the trip myself, and I got so much out of it that I have already booked another one for next year."

Patients do indeed suffer and even die, and we must offer resources and guidance to help clinicians manage and process such stressors. A colleague recently attended the wake of a young man who had died tragically in a car accident. While standing in line to greet the family, she was surprised to see the emergency department physician who had assessed the patient on arrival. She assumed that this physician must be a family friend, given that there had been little time to develop a clinical relationship. The physician explained that he would forever be known as the doctor who signed the death certificate for this patient, and he felt it was important to acknowledge the loss of this young man and the family that survived him.

The physician went on to explain that earlier in his trauma career, he'd distanced himself emotionally from such tragedy and attempted to compartmentalize his work. He'd experienced such intense burnout that he considered leaving his profession, and had long attributed it to the workload and daily frustrations. One day, he realized that his burnout owed primarily to feeling numb in the face of tragedy, not to the workload or frustrations, as bad as those were. From then on, he made a point of acknowledging and engaging with tragedy when it happened. If he had to inform a family that a patient had died, he'd ask about the deceased and what he or she was like as a person. Whenever possible, he attended memorial services for patients even if he'd never personally conversed with them before they died. His shift in approach provided great comfort to families, allowed him to become more present with himself, and enabled him to derive greater meaning from his work.

Healthcare's Added Rewards and Stressors

Most clinicians and caregivers don't aim to eliminate the sources of stress inherent in caring for patients. As Mayo Clinic's Dr. Thomas Howell conveyed in an email communication with one of the authors on May 19, 2019, "As an obstetrician, I know sometimes there are tragic events for patients such as miscarriages, infertility, stillbirths. I know I will give up sleep to tend to deliveries in the middle of the night. I signed up for this." What most clinicians and caregivers would like are reductions in additional stress that exacerbate healthcare's inherent and understandable stressors. "We just have to not make [the inevitable tragedies of caring for patients] harder," Howell continued. "I am not burned out because my job is too hard, I am burned out because it's too hard to do my job."

Sources of stress that are external or incidental to patient care can be both physical and psychological in nature, and can include inadequate staffing, excessive electronic health record (EHR) documentation and charting requirements, a lack of resources, dysfunctional teams, or disruptive colleagues. As mentioned in Chapter 8, a recent Medscape study identified the sources of stress that in their view most contributed to burnout.[8] The top five most frequently selected sources included "too many bureaucratic tasks" (56 percent of respondents), "spending too many hours at work" (39 percent of respondents), lack of respect from colleagues in the work environment (26 percent), the EHR (24 percent), and "insufficient compensation" (24 percent).

Nurses have their own sources of stress. The American Nurses Association's Healthy Nurse, Healthy Nation™ study described workplace stress as the most common safety risk facing nurses, more than twice as prevalent as physical risks related to heavy lifting or injuries from needles and scalpels.[9] More than a quarter of study respondents reported higher workloads than they could manage. Verbal and emotional abuse or bullying was a serious issue for nurses queried, with more than a quarter indicating they'd experienced verbal or physical abuse from a patient or family member in the past year, more than a quarter reporting verbal or nonverbal aggression from peers, and slightly less than a quarter reporting verbal or nonverbal aggression from someone with higher authority.

Some of these causes of stress may create value for patients or the organization, even as they weigh heavily on clinicians. Charting and EHR documentation may promote patient safety while creating administrative fatigue. Adherence to regulatory requirements may be necessary for billing, but it burdens clinicians and reduces the time they have to interact directly with patients or be at home and present with their own families.

Some sources of added stress are just annoyances and frustrations, while others, like bullying, create toxic work environments. Clinicians have a special degree of contempt for elements of their jobs that they perceive as "getting in the way" of good patient care or creating additional safety risks. A neonatal intensive care unit nurse colleague told me of her organization's absolute ban on overtime. This included a seven-minute grace period allowing nurses to complete a final task, log out of their computers, and punch out on-time after the conclusion of a shift. She described an acutely stressful situation she experienced in which she was resting a hand on a patient's wound to secure it, yet had only three minutes to punch out before she would be in trouble. As the seconds ticked away, she remained unsure of whether a nurse would arrive to provide relief.

Traditionally, discussions of burnout historically have focused more on the impact of sources of stress inherent to caregiving, as well as on the compassion fatigue that can result from highly meaningful but stressful work, as opposed to environmental frustrations and annoyances. Unfortunately, current organizational language used to describe burnout often doesn't recognize such changes, rendering many proposed "remedies" poorly matched to the actual sources of stress. Leaders must differentiate between inherent and added stress, as their impacts differ. We might better describe the impact of added stress as causing a caregiver to feel "fed up" rather than burned out. When leaders confuse or conflate these two states, they strike employees as failing to understand the realities of workforce experience. Unlike the stress embedded in the clinical role of patient care, added stress bears no relation to deeper meaning and the emotional rewards that accompany it. We should actively work to reduce added stress so that we are not making it more difficult for clinicians to care for patients.

Added rewards also exist that can make the hard work of patient care even more meaningful. Great teamwork among trusted colleagues, technology, systems that make it easier and safer to care for patients, and recognition of a job well done all enhance workplace satisfaction. Other types of added rewards include benefits, salary, and incentives. While the latter are certainly necessary—benefits must be competitive, and staff should be appropriately compensated—they likely don't change the emotional experience of work or the potential for burnout. People therefore make cognitive trade-offs, choosing to remain in a negative environment for benefits, pay, or staffing. No wonder they experience burnout.

Speaking with clinicians and colleagues, we've found that they tend to intermingle references to frustrations, inefficiencies, toxic work environments, and the blunting of emotion that stems from compartmentalizing the suffering they witness. On the basis of this observation, we've concluded that it's the sum total of rewarding and stressful experiences that determines how employees perceive their work. As unique individuals, people are likely to "tip" at different places due to personality characteristics, career stage, and demands from outside of work. Role choices and specialization also influence tipping points. Flight nurses and emergency medicine physicians, for example, likely have different set points for what they find energizing versus stressful as compared with those who choose primary care.

You don't need to care directly for patients for the model of stress and reward to apply to you. An information technology executive might choose to work in healthcare to contribute to the mission and thereby experience inherent rewards. As a leader in her field, the executive knows that she's ultimately responsible for a functioning system, and this responsibility—which she would feel regardless of the industry in which she works—constitutes a source of stress inherent to her work. But this executive also might encounter sources of added stress particular to her organization, such as lacking funds for critical projects or the presence of a highly political, cantankerous C-suite. Consider, too, a member of the human resources (HR) team who must engage in difficult coaching conversations with staff—an activity that is an inherent part of the role—while also navigating a challenging team environment within his department, a source of added stress. The rewards this HR team member gleans might arise from the potential for career development (added reward) or from the knowledge that his coaching efforts are helping deliver safe, high-quality care for patients (inherent reward).

The Shield of Resilience

Understanding that each of us has a tipping point is well and good, but what determines its location? How can two people experience the same rewards and stress, while only one becomes burned out?

One answer is resilience, a force that changes a person's tipping point, enabling the shouldering of more stress without suffering negative outcomes. We don't mean to suggest that the answer to burnout is increased resilience, enabling organizations to pile additional stress on people. Rather, resilience can serve as a tool that shields you from stress's negative effects and allows you to remain connected to your job's inherent rewards. By enhancing employees' resilience, leaders can help them sustain larger amounts of inherent and environmental stress without reaching their tipping points.

The shield of resilience includes three related parts: a connection to inherent reward, an ability to cope with the inherent stress of patient care, and an ability to withstand the added stress of system demands and dysfunction. To boost resilience to inherent stress, clinicians must learn to avoid compassion fatigue and process events in a way that allows them to stay in touch with caregiving as a meaningful pursuit. By contrast, cultivating resilience to external stress is more around stress management or withstanding suboptimal conditions. Although creating resilience shouldn't be managers' only goal, the difficult work of patient care will always require resilience. We should strive to cultivate nurturing environments that keep caregivers healthy rather than requiring resilience among the workforce so that employees can merely withstand dysfunctional environments.

Cultivating resilience requires that we account for the importance of an employee's particular role. Our research has found that although nurses and physicians have similar levels of activation (the perception of being engaged and feeling effective at work), physicians report lower levels of decompression (the ability to appropriately withdraw and disengage from work). An unpublished study of more than 80,000 healthcare workers—about 19,000 nurses, 5,000 physicians, and 60,000 nonnurse/MD personnel—yielded similar results. Both doctors and nurses reported high and comparable levels of activation. Decompression scores lagged activation for both groups, with physicians reporting more trouble with decompression than their nurse counterparts. Lower scores on resilience measures don't mean a person is deficient at something or that their personal resilience is poor. It is rather a flag that their ability to withstand stress might be in jeopardy.

In addition to differences in the experience of resilience, a related study based on the same data[10] also found evidence that decompression and activation function differently across staff groups. In the overall workforce, both decompression and activation relate to outcomes that are traditionally used to measure workforce engagement, including satisfaction, recommendation of a place for work, recommendation of a place for friends to receive care, and pride in the organization. But the strength of these relationships varies across different groups of staff. For nonclinical staff, activation seems to affect engagement outcomes more than decompression does (a relationship that exists for clinical caregivers as well, although less strongly). Feelings of activation and work fulfillment may thus prove even more critical for nonclinicians, since they might not glean the same level of inherent reward from direct patient-care interactions. This group represents many individuals who could pursue their career in an industry other than healthcare. It may be particularly important for them to connect to healthcare's mission to enhance their engagement in their work.

For clinicians, the significance of activation and decompression seems to hinge on engagement outcome. For both clinician groups, decompression more strongly related to outcomes pertaining to their role as employees, such as overall satisfaction and recommending the organization as a good place to work. Activation was more closely tied than decompression to outcomes related to how the clinicians perceive the organization's overall performance (for example, "I would recommend the organization to friends who needed care" and "I am proud to tell people I work for this organization"). Notably, decompression seems more strongly related to engagement outcomes for nurses than their physician counterparts.

Overall, these findings suggest that while meaningful work matters to everyone, clinicians in general and nurses in particular benefit the most from enhancing their ability to disconnect from work to recharge. But instead of directing individual clinicians to take steps to decompress, we should endeavor to make decompression easier by changing the larger systems in which clinicians work.

A Strategic Approach to Workforce Experience

Organizations can create contexts in which individuals can thrive by focusing on the balance between rewards and stress. We suggest a twofold approach: first, we must address the balance in the work environment by seeking to actively reduce added stress; second, we must enrich individuals' resilience by increasing the connections they feel to inherent rewards, thus helping individuals manage inherent stress.

Reducing Added Stress

Several organizations are already making tangible progress in reducing added stress associated with workload. One group of researchers analyzed organizational efforts to reduce the burden on clinicians, identifying activities (such as follow-up communication, reviewing and responding to post-appointment lab results, and documenting after-visit summaries) that lead to increased hours of clinician work per day.[11] These researchers described new processes and protocols that would reduce or eliminate these tasks, including colocating physicians and medical assistants to enhance communication, scheduling lab tests before patient visits, and pairing nurses with physicians to scribe notes during care interactions.

Organizations can lower added stress by streamlining technology and promoting the fabric of relationships. An innovative program at Hawaii Pacific Health, appropriately called Get Rid of Stupid Stuff (GROSS), asks staff to identify steps in processes that add no value and that the organization could easily eliminate.[12] "Value" implies a high bar, as activities nominated for "elimination" must not be necessary for patient safety, regulatory requirements, reimbursement, patient-centeredness, or staff engagement. To date, leaders have considered more than 150 submissions, and the idea that the system is willing and interested in reducing daily frustrations appears to have captured staff members' imagination.

Leaders at Emory have taken a different approach, implementing the "Emory Healthcare Pledge" that clarifies the expectations of respectful collegial behavior and allows staff and physicians to hold themselves accountable for contributing to a positive team environment.[13] By establishing standards and commitment, the pledge lowers the chances that colleagues will overlook disrespectful behavior, grants them permission to speak up, and inspires colleagues to be their best selves.

No matter which tactics leaders embrace to address external causes of stress, we recommend that they follow a consistent approach. It's not enough to reduce or eliminate an external source of stress—you must publicize that you are doing so. Conversely, although organizations can't eliminate or reduce some sources of stress, publicly acknowledging the challenges they face might nonetheless help. Begin by naming each source of stress, using language that reflects the experiences of those enduring the stress. For instance, you might state that, "It is too complicated to order a flu shot for my patients through the electronic health record." If you can eliminate this source of stress, make sure to follow up and do so. If you can only reduce it, take that action, and again, let people know you are doing so. In the rare event that you can neither eliminate nor reduce a source of stress, acknowledge this and also describe the efforts you've undertaken.

The following flowchart (Figure 9.1) can help you explore sources of stress and arrive at helpful actions to take. A team at one organization used it to learn that employees didn't like the color-coded scrubs they had to wear. Through follow-up discussions, they also discovered that staff resented that they had to purchase new uniforms themselves. Staff had voted on their preferred color, but leaders overruled them, leaving them feeling powerless. Another organization used this flowchart to identify a communications gap related to the rollout of their patient portal. Leaders had required the staff to wear buttons with the slogan, "Ask Me About Our Patient Portal," but gave them no training or guidance. As a result, staff didn't know how to answer patient questions. When training finally did occur, it didn't relate the content back to the buttons staffers were required to wear. This didn't represent a source of stress on par with a patient dying, but it was significant nonetheless.

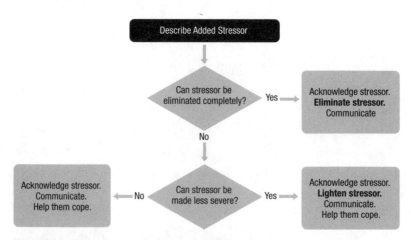

Figure 9.1   Addressing Added Environmental Stressors

Enhancing Resilience

To enhance resilience, leaders should remind employees of patient care's inherent rewards, help them cope with the impact of inherent stress, and develop resources that allow employees to cope with added environmental stress. Mayo Clinic emphasizes the presence of inherent reward by funding dinner outings for physicians so as to foster conversation and fellowship.[14] This measure has lowered burnout and boosted "collegiality, connection and meaning in work." The promotion of teamwork appears to help connect staff with the inherent reward of a cooperative care environment. Even without paying for meals, organizations can amplify patient care's inherent rewards by emphasizing the goal of reducing patient suffering and promoting patient safety, since both tap into clinicians' and caregivers' intrinsic desires.

Organizations can also enhance resilience by giving employees the tactics, skills, and support required to withstand the stress inherent in their clinical role, while also acknowledging the difficulty of the work. Atrium Health maintains a network of "compassion champions" who personally commit to exercising compassion with themselves, their team, and beyond.[15] These champions support the organization's Code Lavender program that deploys rapid response emotional support after a traumatic event. Colleagues can call a Code Lavender after patient deaths, violence toward employees, or other moments when people feel unsafe. Atrium's flagship hospital averages eight Code Lavenders per day. Each time, the hospital offers direct personal support via hospital chaplains, nurse supervisors, and employee assistance program (EAP) representatives.

A third step organizations can take to help team members cope with added stress is to promote clinician and caregiver well-being and generalized stress-reduction techniques. Many organizations promote proper diet and exercise as ways to cope with stress,[16] though this hardly excuses leaders from neglecting environmental factors. Mindfulness, gratitude, and yoga are also effective, but leaders shouldn't turn to them as primary strategies unless system-wide efforts to address added stress and inherent rewards are also in place.

Conclusion

A friend who recently lost her father to a series of medical errors spent time with him in the ICU during his final days and found that she particularly appreciated the support of Aiko, a nurse who worked the night shift. Aiko (not her real name) was kind, compassionate, and fiercely competent in monitoring her patients, strategizing about the administration of medications to avoid interactions, and calculating precise dosages. She advocated tirelessly for patient safety, calling the lab to follow up when tests did not return on time, and pleading when critical-care patients were at risk as a result. Although her 12-hour shift ended at 7:00 A.M., she routinely stayed at her computer for another three hours to complete documentation tasks.

As my friend's relationship with Aiko developed, she learned more about her, including her recent loss of her husband and father. Aiko mentioned that she didn't think she could endure being a nurse for much longer and mused that she'd love to work down in the gift shop. As my friend's father declined, Aiko cried with the family and offered support. When he passed, she stayed more than four hours after her shift ended to sit with them. "Is this why you don't want to be a nurse anymore?" my friend asked. To her surprise, Aiko said no—this was part of her job, and although it made her sad, it didn't make her want to leave. It was the "other stuff" that frustrated her because it got in the way of her job.

If you occupy a leadership role in a healthcare organization, please take stories like Aiko's to heart. Know that Aiko is both engaged *and* potentially burned out. She understands her role's importance and feels privileged to be able to care for patients. Although her role is inherently stressful, she can handle it, because she can connect the stress to what makes her job meaningful. Her personal circumstances outside of work certainly affect her tipping point's location, but the added stress has become unbearable, and she's desperate for a way out. A well-intentioned but misguided organization might offer her a stress-reduction class or recommend wellness tactics like good nutrition or better sleep hygiene. But we can see how Aiko would perceive that message as dismissive of her pain and unhelpful.

The framework we've suggested in this chapter will prompt organizations to take more specific action at all levels to improve both work environment and employee experience. There is no universal approach to apply; particular inputs of reward and stress will vary by staff group, as will the components of resilience. To reduce the potential for burnout, differentiate between inherent and added sources of stress, and manage each appropriately, with a strong emphasis on communication. Contextualize the nature of resilience so that staff don't feel responsible for their own burnout. Try to reconnect staff to the rewards inherent in their jobs to help them cope with inherent stress and with any added stressors that remain. Over time, balancing rewards and stress will allow you to build a workforce of people who feel proud about what they do and where they work, and who are committed to providing compassionate, high-quality care.

IN SUM

- Resilience is critical, yet healthcare leaders generally don't understand or manage it very well.
- Resilience isn't the antidote to burnout. Leaders must seek to *prevent* burnout through optimizing work environments.
- To address workplace issues, we should distinguish between sources of stress that are inherent to patient care and those that derive from the particular work context, addressing each appropriately.
- Bolstering resilience helps shield individuals from stress so that they can manage burnout's potentially negative effects.
- To enhance resilience, leaders must help employees remain connected to the meaning of their work, effectively deal with inherent sources of stress, and find healthy ways to cope with stress and frustration stemming from external causes.

10 | The Virtuous Cycle

*Craig Clapper, PE, CMQ/OE, and
Steve Kreiser, CDR (USN Ret.), MBA*

> *Most so-called improvement efforts have merely
> undercut one domain—whether safety, quality, patient
> experience, caregiver engagement, or efficiency—to
> enhance another. This chapter discusses how healthcare
> organizations can use safety culture—both patient
> and workforce safety—and High Reliability to produce
> caregiver engagement and make progress across all
> domains simultaneously.*

ON MAY 14, 2019, June Altaras stood on a convention center platform gazing out on 1,000 leaders from MultiCare, a healthcare system in Washington and Idaho. Since joining MultiCare as senior vice president and chief quality, safety, and nursing officer, Altaras had led the organization's safety culture transformation team, much as she had as a nursing leader at Swedish Medical Center in Seattle and as an administrator at Providence St. Joseph Health throughout the West. Now, under the leadership of MultiCare's president and chief executive officer (CEO), Bill Robertson, all of the system leaders had convened to discuss their safety culture transformation plans.

"Who here is a patient who was harmed in their care?" Altaras asked her large group.

A few leaders stood.

"Who here has a family member who was harmed as a patient?"

Again, many leaders stood.

"And who here has been involved in the harming of a patient as a clinical or administrative leader?"

Everyone in the room was now standing, because virtually everyone knew of a patient who was harmed.

The leaders at MultiCare are not alone. Patient harm is endemic in healthcare. According to a 1997 estimate, upward of 98,000 patients die every year due to errors in their care,[1] a number that has since risen to more than a quarter million. Incredibly, patient harm is now the third leading cause of death in the United States following cancer and heart disease. One patient in every 1,000 admitted to a hospital will die because of medical error.

Our caregivers suffer as well. In the United States, workforce safety in healthcare—both rates of injury and time lost to injury—is poor compared to other key industries like agriculture, mining, construction, manufacturing, transportation, and utilities. Even such dangerous work as high steel construction or logging is safer than healthcare. Table 10.1 shows the Bureau of Labor Statistics (BLS) tabulation of Total Case Incident Rate (TCIR) and Days Away, Restricted, or Transferred (DART) rate for the US healthcare industry in 2017. Only in numbers of fatalities does healthcare perform better in workforce safety, and with an increase in workplace violence, healthcare is unfortunately closing that gap. In hospitals, 6 out of every 100 caregivers are injured each year. Two out of these six receive such severe injuries that they can't work, sometimes for the day and other times for the rest of their lives. Overall, poor safety costs US healthcare companies about $13 billion each year.[2]

Table 10.1   Harm Statistics for Healthcare

Healthcare Setting	TCIR	DART
Ambulance service	7.1	4.1
Nursing home	6.3	3.8
Hospital	5.7	2.3
Ambulatory	2.5	0.9

Zero is the only acceptable number for workforce and patient harm. Although all healthcare leaders want harm and injury in the workplace to end, many don't realize that patient and workforce safety owe directly to caregiver engagement, nor do they regard patient harm reduction measures as cost-effective. In truth, the connection between workplace safety and caregiver engagement is quite robust, forming a *virtuous cycle* of cause-and-effect relationships. In Figure 10.1 (see next page), engagement of the caregiver and safety culture (both patient and workforce safety) appears at the 9 o'clock position. Safety produces engagement, and in return caregiver engagement produces safety. These two variables work together to produce clinical quality. And safety, engagement, and quality are thus all integral to patient experience. We cannot improve patient experience without improving safety and quality, and healthcare leaders who don't understand this labor in vain.

Improving efficiency in the virtuous cycle is a little more complex and requires an understanding of reliability. Reliability refers to the probability that the work system will function correctly for patients. Reliability is an *emergent property* of the work system in that it arises out of the interaction among all parts of the system: the people, process, protocol, technology, environment of care, and so on. To achieve safety, engagement, quality, and patient

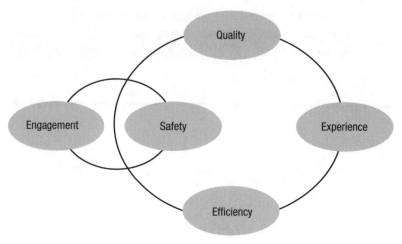

Figure 10.1   The Virtuous Cycle

experience, we must have a High Reliability work system in place. If not, we see unwanted variation in how care is delivered, with poor outcomes as a result. The presence of High Reliability also enables the virtuous cycle to improve efficiency. Healthcare leaders should thus use robust performance improvement to relentlessly drive dysfunction out of care delivery systems, rendering them safer and more efficient.

The Nexus of Safety and Engagement

Let's take a closer look at the relationship between safety and employee engagement. Our survey data indicate that employees who report feeling safe and who report that they would feel safe as a patient in their units are more engaged. Caregivers expect safety, and excellence in this area likewise allows them to perceive their work as meaningful and valuable. Conversely, common injuries like overexertion in patient handling, slips and trips, and potential exposures from needlesticks or fluid splashes and the terrifying injuries of workplace violence reduce caregivers' ability to achieve great outcomes. Caregivers must also feel protected from psychological harm. They must feel safe to advocate for their patients, ask questions, provide feedback to other caregivers without judgment, and suggest improvements to practices without others seeing them as "disruptive."

Everybody wins when caregivers feel safe and become more engaged in their work. Engaged caregivers in turn become more resilient, investing more in practices that keep their patients and teammates safe, paying more attention, and communicating more frequently and with greater clarity. They also think more cautiously, follow protocols more closely, and seek help more often. Engaged caregivers are also more likely to invest in improvement activities for the work and care delivery system, improving safety, clinical quality, patient experience, and efficiency.

As leaders, the best way to initiate a virtuous cycle of safety and engagement is to invest in a few key cultural and organizational elements. First, cultivate mutual respect in the workplace, using safety culture and High Reliability Organizing (HRO) strategies to nurture a sense of psychological safety. Second, use safety culture and HRO strategies to help caregivers prioritize safety and patients, thus making their work feel more meaningful to them. And third, streamline work systems, using daily improvement systems to fix problems that prevent caregivers from doing their jobs the way they love to.

While safety culture and engagement surveys consistently affirm the close, mutually affirming relationship between safety and engagement, safety leaders tend to articulate such insights even more forcefully. Drs. Rich Brilli and Terry Davis of Nationwide Children's Hospital in Columbus, Ohio, are patient safety innovators. Nationwide was the first pediatric hospital to proclaim Zero Harm as the only right number for the organization. Nationwide was likewise the first to post its serious safety event rate, a measure of preventable patient harm, on the web for the community to see, and to prioritize patient safety and workforce safety equally. As a result, Nationwide has seen a 90 percent reduction in patient harm events over 10 years, and a 75 percent reduction in workforce injury, leading in turn to engagement gains. As Brilli reflects, "People feel valued for the work they do, and us valuing their safety engages our people in safety and quality." "People are jazzed by safety," Davis says. "They come to work to make kids better. When kids get hurt—no one wants that; people rally around that easily."[3]

Safety Culture Transformation

How do organizations like Nationwide implement the three key elements described previously to improve safety, and in turn, engagement? Outside of the healthcare industry, safety management systems (SMSs) help translate injury and accident reduction goals into tactical activities. SMSs are poised to achieve similar outcomes in healthcare, and can encompass policy, plans and procedures, culture, promotional activities, and learning programs. An SMS targeted to workforce safety in healthcare is shown in Figure 10.2. Let's take a brief look at each of its key elements in turn.

Policy and Procedure

Organizations must clearly articulate their commitment to patient and worker safety in their corporate mission and vision statements. Organizations must also publicly proclaim safety goals and policies designed to reduce patient and worker injuries to zero. In 2012 Jim Skogsbergh, the president and CEO of Advocate Health Care in Chicago (now Advocate Aurora Health), set a goal of

Policy	Safety Culture	Safety Promotion	Learning Systems
Safety statement	HRO leader skills	Hazard-specific prevention	Injury measures
Zero injury goal	Universal skills (error prevention)	Safety absolutes (Red Rules)	Safety action teams (inset)
Just culture	Collegiality (relationship skills)	Lessons learned	Safety culture measure
	Personal safety assessment tools	Artifacts (posters)	Local learning systems
			Cause analysis
			Common cause analysis
			Self-assessment of program
			Independent assessment of program
			Operating experience

Safety Action Teams

1. Slips, trips, and falls
2. Repetitive motion
3. Workforce violence
4. Blood/body fluid exposures
5. Safe patient handling

Figure 10.2   Workforce Safety Management System

reaching zero patient harm by 2020. Some people called this his "moon shot," invoking John F. Kennedy's goal of landing on the moon by 1969. To achieve this goal, Skogsbergh crafted a strategic plan with supporting policies. Seven years later, Advocate Aurora achieved a stunning 60 percent reduction in serious events of preventable harm. As this book goes to press, Advocate Aurora hasn't yet achieved zero, but has broadened its focus to include worker harm reduction. Still, its inspiring vision and mission continues to engage team members throughout the organization, while its steady progress has resulted in hundreds of saved lives.

Safety Culture

An organization's culture consists of a shared vision and commonly held values, often reinforced and bolstered by actions, including those taken when others aren't looking. While organizations have trouble measuring culture as such, several leading and lagging indicators can help us gauge how stakeholders *perceive* it. Patient safety surveys, such as the Agency for Healthcare Research and Quality (AHRQ) culture of safety survey or the Press Ganey safety culture survey, provide valuable information about how team members perceive safety indicators, including how much leaders support safety, employees' comfort level in communicating safety concerns, and how much they trust that leaders will respond fairly to instances of human error. Organizations can also assess culture's efficacy from a safety standpoint by analyzing previous safety events to spot recurring individual and systemic failures. This multidimensional Pareto analysis, also known as a common cause analysis, can provide a dataset of individual and system influences that lead to patient harm events. In a 2016 comparison database of over 4,800 unique errors and contributing factors, culture represented the largest system factor (Figure 10.3).

Culture in this analysis includes people and their interactions, as well as such organizational staples as corporate mission, vision, and values; collaboration among professional groups; operational accountability; and reliable practice habits in the overall environment. In a safety-focused culture, organizational policy and procedural expectations align well with safety. Everyone understands the practices and behaviors deemed acceptable and safe (sometimes called "universal skills").

"How" Data		"Why" Data	
People Causes	HPI*Compare* (%)	System Causes	HPI*Compare* (%)
Knowledge and skill	15.1	Structure (job design)	10.7
Attention on task	11.4	Culture (people and people interaction)	53.0
Information processing	9.6	Process	16.8
Critical thinking	39.7	Policy and protocol	12.5
Noncompliance	17.8	Technology and environment	7.0
Normalized deviance	6.3	Acts coded for system cause	68.9
Acts coded for human error	52.9	*Culture Preventable =*	73.0
Comparison based on 4,868 inappropriate acts from 120 sites in HPI CCA database			

Figure 10.3   HPI Comparison Dataset of Individual and System Causes of Patient Harm Events

While healthcare professionals are usually technically skilled in their specialties, most lack universal skills, including the ability to communicate well, improve situational awareness and decision-making, and overcome distractions, interruptions, and fatigue. Figure 10.4 conveys the kinds of standard universal skills needed to build and sustain reliability on the part of clinical and nonclinical staff, leaders, and physicians. The tools listed on the left are evidence-based, shown to reduce human error and events of harm across industries in general and in healthcare in particular by as much as 80 percent. The behaviors listed on the right, which represent a version of the service behaviors discussed in this book's Introduction, help improve collegiality between coworkers. Such "tones," as we call them, help employees overcome cultural hesitations to speak up, ask questions, or identify errors on the part of coworkers.

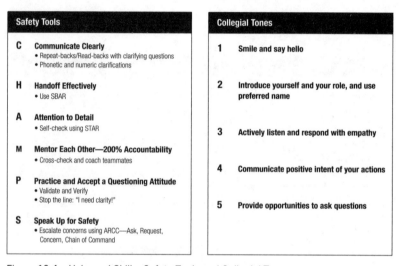

Safety Tools	Collegial Tones
C Communicate Clearly • Repeat-backs/Read-backs with clarifying questions • Phonetic and numeric clarifications	**1** Smile and say hello
H Handoff Effectively • Use SBAR	**2** Introduce yourself and your role, and use preferred name
A Attention to Detail • Self-check using STAR	**3** Actively listen and respond with empathy
M Mentor Each Other—200% Accountability • Cross-check and coach teammates	**4** Communicate positive intent of your actions
P Practice and Accept a Questioning Attitude • Validate and Verify • Stop the line: "I need clarity!"	**5** Provide opportunities to ask questions
S Speak Up for Safety • Escalate concerns using ARCC—Ask, Request, Concern, Chain of Command	

Figure 10.4   Universal Skills: Safety Tools and Collegial Tones

In the absence of structured leadership efforts, an organization can never translate desired behaviors such as these into practice habits. Leaders should thus adopt a set of practices to reinforce the message of safety first, to find and fix system problems that prevent people from performing effectively, and to hold others accountable for meeting behavioral expectations. These leadership skills, typical among High Reliability Organizations (HROs), include daily safety huddles, structured and purposeful rounding, and a fair and just implementation structure to allow the organization to respond to errors and mistakes consistently.

Safety Promotion

Safety efforts must span your entire organization, from the C-suite's electronic messages, to meeting agendas across the organization, visual mechanisms like posters, badge cards, intranet sites, and videos, and the sharing of both safety success stories and lessons learned from harm events or injuries. The goal of safety promotion is to raise people's awareness of risk and reduce complacency about the potential of harm throughout healthcare organizations. In HROs, leaders consciously promote safe practices and behavioral expectations around safety, and they speak openly about injuries, harm, and risky behaviors.

Learning Systems

Key to all SMSs are activities necessary to make learning a norm within the organization. So-called learning organizations inculcate a "mess up, fess up" approach, encouraging members to speak up and report errors and system problems. Such an approach allows for the measurement, study, and correction of errors, events, injuries, and harm levels as well as the establishment of control loops to continuously improve outcomes. Control loops require leaders to monitor outcomes via metrics of success, determine gaps in performance from expectations and benchmarks based on those metrics, create action plans designed to close the gaps, and then monitor the corrective actions to completion.

"Mess up, fess up" also helps leaders analyze safety events to uncover links between individual human error and elements of the system that might have contributed, allowing them to better determine corrective actions. For example, organizations can develop and deploy local learning systems at the unit and department levels to engage frontline staff in identifying and solving problems. As more problems are identified and solved, staff recognize the organization's commitment to building a system that can deliver safe, reliable care to patients and allow staff to return home safely at the end of their workdays.

Yale New Haven Health is a multihospital system headquartered in New Haven, Connecticut. By implementing an SMS that includes daily leadership safety huddles, structured leadership rounds, a fair and just culture, universal skills to prevent human error, and a strong cause analysis program, Yale New Haven has reduced serious safety events by over 80 percent. According to Katie O'Leary, executive director for safety and quality, the 200 operational leaders and 25 physicians who volunteered to become safety trainers have helped shape their culture of safety, training 22,000 staff members in six months. One physician, Dr. Al Friedman, still walks half a mile between campuses every two weeks to train new staff members and residents as part of orientation. This commitment to safety, taught and modeled by leaders, demonstrates to staff that the organization is committed to safety as one of its core values.

According to Dr. Tom Balcezak, chief medical officer for Yale New Haven Health System, the organization's employees and the medical staff have found safety to be a great cultural unifier. In 2012, during the merger of two large hospitals, leadership wanted to ensure that neither legacy organization felt like the conqueror or conquered. A focus on safety brought the two hospitals together; everyone felt strongly about the mission of providing safe patient care. As Balcezak affirms, it was critical that leaders create an environment in which psychological safety wasn't just talked about but owned and supported by leaders. That started at morning leadership safety briefs, meetings at which leaders and staff openly discuss safety issues to learn from them. The overall results have been impressive. In Yale New Haven's AHRQ culture of safety survey, every single domain has improved since the organization began focusing on safety and reliability. Error and event reporting has doubled, with a greater focus on near-miss events.

Deploying an SMS

To activate the virtuous cycle of safety and engagement, we must deploy all SMS strategies across our organizations. This in turn requires that we develop, implement, and inculcate additional leadership skills typically found in HROs to convey the importance of safety, reinforce expectations around safe practices, and address and fix those problems that affect how frontline staff perform. Let's briefly review each of these areas in turn.

Safety Messaging Using Three-Part Storytelling

When Paul O'Neill took the helm at Alcoa in 1987, he started his first shareholders' meeting not by speaking about typical business concerns like finances or taxes, but by focusing on the importance of every Alcoa worker's safety. O'Neill set a goal of zero workforce injuries, prompting his colleagues to think that he had gone a bit crazy. But employee safety was something that everyone in the organization could support, including workers, union leaders, frontline managers, and executives. O'Neill's focus on promoting low-risk behaviors and system improvements throughout Alcoa's worldwide operations helped identify defects that negatively impacted operations. As Alcoa started to see improvements in safety, it also started to recognize improvements in performance, leading to record-high profits.[4] O'Neill understood a simple truth about organizations: good systems are *safe* systems.

Healthcare leaders should foster engagement by taking a page from O'Neill's playbook and reinforcing a safety-first mind-set in their organizations. At Sentara Healthcare, a 12-hospital integrated system headquartered in Norfolk, Virginia, all meetings across the organization start with a safety message, demonstrating Sentara's commitment to the issue. Leaders have adopted a three-part structure for telling safety-related stories that helps clarify and reinforce the message. Stories start with an introduction of their purpose; they provide concise detail around a plot, conflict, and resolution; and they conclude by delivering a clear lesson for all to take away and apply.

In April 2019, a leader at one of Sentara's hospitals shared the following story about patient protection. Note how the story follows this three-part structure and highlights some of the universal and HRO leader skills detailed in the SMS.

> I am going to share a safety moment with you that highlights the importance of utilizing High Reliability tools such as preoccupation with failure, consistent questioning, teamwork, and elevating safety to a precondition of operations, given that even one mistake or system breakdown can have tragic consequences.
>
> Susan, a physician's assistant and mother of three, came to the Sentara Virginia Beach Emergency Department complaining of pain in a finger that she had cut with a knife two days prior. She was admitted to the hospital, and after she made three trips to the OR to drain her bursa, the wound was still not healing. Her physicians diagnosed her with necrotizing fasciitis, a serious condition that leads to the death of one in three people afflicted.

Preoccupied with failure, the care team collaborated on what additional treatment might benefit the patient, and recommended hyperbaric treatment at Sentara Leigh Hospital. Teams from both hospitals communicated clearly and handed off effectively to ensure an efficient and timely emergency transport to Sentara Leigh for hyperbaric treatment. When the patient was on the way to the OR for a fourth drainage, nurses from the ICU paid attention to detail, noticing the patient had poor oxygen levels. Anticipating potential problems, they planned ahead to ensure the patient came back from the OR on a ventilator. Seven days later, surgeons completed an arm wound closure, and the patient returned to the ICU.

Medical professionals discharged Susan 22 days after her admission, and she was able to return home to live a full life with her husband and three children, counting among the 33 percent of patients who survive necrotizing fasciitis. Because of the dedication of two separate hospital care teams and the intentional use of HRO principles and the Sentara safety habits, Susan had a positive outcome and an exceptional patient experience.

Leaders at Sentara understand that the best stories are a brief two to three minutes in length. Minds wander when overloaded with information, but a well-told story holds people's attention and helps engage caregivers by connecting them back to their work's higher purpose. Numbers can numb our conscious and jargon can jar our ability to focus attention, but stories can create a vivid and stimulating vision of a positive future while inspiring and engaging others. Leaders who tell stories in this succinct, three-part format can better engage their people to meet safety, quality, or experience of care goals.

Leader Rounding Using a 4C Structure

A naval aircraft carrier is a floating city, home to over 5,000 people of diverse backgrounds and responsibilities. When conducting operations in environments like the Mediterranean Sea or Arabian Gulf, personnel work above, on, and below the flight deck in a highly coordinated and safety-focused effort. While those working in this complex, high-risk environment make the work of launching, recovering, refueling, loading ordinance, and relaunching jets look easy, the work is fraught with hidden dangers that can quickly result in a tragedy absent airtight policies and procedures. How are leaders able to instill a commitment to policy and procedural compliance, especially in an environment where the average age is 20? A consistent leadership presence in the operating environment helps, as does talking about expectations, proactively identifying barriers to compliance, and clearly asking for commitment actions.

In healthcare, we can achieve similar consistencies, bolstering the quality of care delivery as well as engagement levels, if leaders model consistent rounding practices in the operating environment. Leaders who regularly observe workforce behaviors, discuss expectations, seek barriers to compliance, and ask for commitments develop higher levels of accountability and ultimately achieve better outcomes, leaving employees happier and more engaged. We can describe, teach, and coach this type of rounding to hospital leadership teams using the following 4C structure:

- Create a connection: share a story or metric about the importance of the topic on which you are rounding.

- Check for can-dos: assess general knowledge and understanding of expectations.

- Collect concerns: ask for potential barriers to staff meeting expectations.

- Call for commitment: remove any ambiguity by asking employees for a personal commitment to help achieve organizational goals and meet specific expectations.

Dr. Christopher Trotz, executive medical director for the 150 locations of Inspira Medical Group in southern New Jersey, is especially skilled in rounding in this manner. When talking to a care team at a physician practice site about medication lists for patients transitioning to skilled nursing facilities, Trotz effectively conveyed the issue's relevance for safety, shared the shocking rates of patient harm during transitions of care, and talked about effective strategies for reconciling medication lists. To keep the conversation focused and on track, Trotz structured his conversation around the "4Cs." First, he "connected" with the care team by relaying specific problems from their own network. He then asked about what they thought the team "can do" to reduce medication events and asked if they had any "concerns" about the solutions he was promoting. He then specifically asked for their "commitment." All leaders should use these 4Cs while on rounds to promote specific safety behaviors and engagement while building and reinforcing accountability.

Using the 4C influencer tool as part of their HRO leader skills, Trotz and his fellow safety leaders have led Inspira to a 79 percent reduction in serious preventable patient harm and a 49 percent reduction in workforce injury. And the culture and engagement survey results for their organization show similar improvement. Across Trotz's medical group, safety culture has improved by 35 percent and engagement by 2 percent. As Trotz advises, "Caregivers and providers are interested in getting their patients better. Use the 4Cs to identify problems that stand between them and the care they love."[5]

Local Learning Using Learning Boards to Fix System Headaches

Local learning systems (Figure 10.5) are large, visual displays erected in high-traffic, public areas of a unit or department. Leaders use them to identify systemic, safety-related issues at the local level and to provide a mechanism for unit leaders and staff members to implement solutions together. Properly used, a local learning board helps employees understand problems as opportunities for improvement. These boards display new problems, issues that the team is currently working on, and previously identified problems that the team has solved. Leaders encourage team members to use the learning board by recognizing issues on the "new problem" portion as good news and thanking staff members for bringing the problems to management's attention. Leaders and staff then collaborate to prioritize problem-solving, moving select items to the "working" category by forming teams and creating action plans to track and ultimately resolve problems.

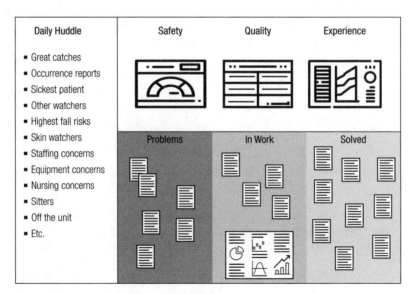

Figure 10.5   Local Learning System

As a learning board becomes part of a unit's daily routine, teams can detect potential problems early, resolving these problems before they can compromise patient care. The team then celebrates these resolutions, transitioning them to the "solved" portion of the learning board and delivering positive feedback to those involved. Such positive leader feedback creates a sense of accomplishment that will naturally lead team members to become more engaged. Learning boards work well to create an environment of transparency, especially combined with daily, unit-based huddles and publicly posted departmental safety measures. Team members openly share data around safety, quality, and experience, creating a "burning platform" that supports change efforts. As they huddle around the local learning system each day to conduct the unit-level safety huddle, all team members can identify discrepancies between current and desired performance. The shared understanding of problems and the presence of experts at the front line helping generate solutions create ownership, inspiring the team to excellence.

Universal Skills for Leaders, Staff, and Medical Staff

To further reduce errors and harm events for patients and workers, and to help build employee engagement, organizations should design a set of simple, habitual, and universally applicable evidence-based tools along the lines of Figure 10.4. Reliability skills, sometimes referred to as nontechnical skills, are very effective in improving human performance, and most healthcare organizations that have integrated them into their everyday culture have reduced serious safety events by an average of 80 percent. Organizations in other industries have used such strategies for decades, achieving similar results.

One tool, validate and verify, is a thinking skill for a questioning attitude that allows caregivers and teams to make sense of incomplete and incorrect information. This technique ranked first among 20 critical-thinking tools analyzed in the nuclear power industry in the 1980s and 1990s. The aviation industry has long used another tool called repeat-back, a spoken communication tool where senders and receivers confirm information, as well as phonetic and numeric clarifications where senders and receivers confirm sound-alike names and numbers to avoid communication errors. A 1982 study demonstrated that the STAR technique—where caregivers stop for one second to think before they act—reduced skill-based errors by 90 percent. Still another tool, effective peer checking between care providers, can reduce error rates by 99.99 percent! Details about these skills can be found in our recent book *Zero Harm*. To achieve such dramatic error reduction, however, employees must habitually practice and discuss these tools, committing to them as an essential part of the organization's safety culture.

The way organizational members interact, engage, and communicate with one another likewise is critical for long-term cultural transformation. To flatten organizational hierarchies, help people feel more comfortable speaking up and asking questions, and develop more positive work environments, organizations should adopt a version of the service behaviors discussed in this book's Introduction and highlighted in Figure 10.4.

Smiling and greeting fellow team members, patients, and families should be mandatory for everyone in a healthcare organization. Disclosing your name and role to patients and caregivers unfamiliar to your team helps establish familiarity and trust. Active, empathetic listening allows you to identify with others on a personal level—not just hearing what others say, but truly understanding and processing information they present. Demonstrating the positive intent of one's actions helps reduce the misperceptions that can sometimes result from unintentional nonverbal interactions, such as multitasking, facial expressions, emotional reactions, or body language. Finally, the best communicators provide opportunities for others to ask questions and seek to eliminate hesitation or fear. When practiced consistently, these relationship behaviors bolster teamwork and interpersonal relationships, increasing patient and worker safety, bolstering workforce engagement, and ultimately enhancing patient experience, work-unit efficiency, and financial vitality.

Just Culture

An essential element of any SMS is what many safety experts call "just culture," an organizational commitment to responding to errors, events, and performance variations in a fair, consistent, and just manner. More than simply a decision-making algorithm or support tool, just culture requires organizational sanction via clear policy and supporting documents. Human resources (HR) professionals must become just culture experts, providing consistent support to operational leaders as they respond to events. Operational leaders in turn must receive training in just culture principles and become skilled in their application.

Staff and physicians who commit errors or mistakes must know that they will receive fair and consistent treatment. If they feel unfairly punished, then it becomes less likely that they will report an error, and their engagement will understandably decline. This in turn compromises the team's ability to identify system issues or failed defensive barriers that contributed to the event. When staff feel physiologically unsafe to speak up or report because they fear punishment, repercussion, or retaliation, it not only affects the safety of the system but adversely affects organizational culture and ultimately workforce engagement.

Leaders have an obligation to create an environment grounded in a fair and just culture so that every member of the organization feels safe to speak up, report errors or system problems, pose questions, or voice concerns. Leaders must emphasize that staff are empowered and expected to speak up, and that they won't tolerate harassment of those who do. If leaders hear rumors of staff retaliation, they must address them immediately by referring the problem to HR or taking disciplinary action. Difficult conversations with certain medical staff might become necessary, but the message such responses communicate about the preeminence of safety is worth it. Even if a safety concern is ultimately unfounded, organizations must recognize and reward people for their willingness to speak up. Over time, speaking up won't require nearly as much courage, because safety concerns have become so deeply embedded in the organization's culture.

Measurement and Control Loops

When Navy pilots land aboard an aircraft carrier at sea, leaders debrief each pilot about the landing, providing them in-depth, graded, and face-to-face feedback. Grades are posted in every squadron ready room to measure and improve performance, and leaders expect pilots to use such feedback to improve their landings. This measurement, feedback, and corrective action cycle is known as a control loop. For healthcare organizations to improve performance, they must also measure it, provide consistent feedback, and identify and implement corrective actions.

One pitfall that adversely affects healthcare organizations is the duplication of measurement, which can lead to uncoordinated cycles of improvement for leaders and team members. Numerous measures of harm exist in healthcare, yet some fail to identify preventability or causality, while others don't establish clear criteria for the effects of known healthcare complications that can lead to a bad outcome. As discussed in Chapter 5, many organizations conduct multiple surveys of their staff, physicians, and leaders with respect to safety, engagement, resilience, and burnout, causing survey fatigue. Leaders should measure these different elements together and develop action plans around a single improvement cycle, as is possible using Press Ganey's "One Ask" culture and engagement survey. Leaders should also create a dashboard of performance indicators that provides leading, real-time, and lagging measures of safety performance along with control loops that drive feedback and corrective actions designed to improve performance over time.

Conclusion

In just a few short years, one large health system we work with achieved an approximate reduction of 42 percent in lost-time injuries. Leaders spent time identifying hazards and systematically reducing risks to workers, based on data and stakeholder listening sessions. They deployed processes, methods, and tools, and clarified expectations around the use of lift devices to reduce back injuries and nonslip footwear to reduce slips, trips, and falls. They promoted the use of universal skills, like being accountable and speaking up for safety, as guiding behaviors. Patient handling injuries at their largest hospital dropped by 53 percent, needlesticks dropped by 24 percent, and workers' compensation costs dropped by 40 percent from reductions in workplace violence injuries. Slips, trips, and falls dropped by 13 percent. Feedback from staff was extremely positive; they found it refreshing to hear leadership vocalize that their safety was considered just as important as patient safety.

These reductions in workforce injuries were not only good for the safety and engagement of staff at this organization, but for business. Cost savings accruing from the focus on worker safety from 2014 to 2018 averaged over $1.6 million per year. This is the ultimate goal of High Reliability Organizing and leaders who make it a reality: keeping people safe as part of an overall strategy to provide exceptional care to patients.

IN SUM

- Organizations achieve Zero Harm and zero injury by deploying systems of safety consistently over time.
- Safety science provides safety leaders with the organizational structure, processes, protocols, environment of care, and technological interfaces necessary for safety.
- Safety yields higher engagement, and vice versa. Use safety and engagement to produce clinical quality, patient experience, efficiency, and continuous improvement in the virtuous cycle.
- To enhance safety and caregiver engagement, create a safety culture that promotes mutual respect and meaningful work, using local learning systems to fix work system headaches.

Transforming Experience

11

Rachel Biblow and Martin Wright

All too often, healthcare organizations regard improvements to safety, quality, patient experience, and employee engagement as separate and distinct efforts. As organizations more broadly define "patient experience" to include all of these elements, they must develop strategies for transforming care delivery and creating engaging cultures. By endeavoring to offer the best experiences for our patients, we build engagement by reconnecting caregivers with why they got into healthcare in the first place: to care for others.

CENTRAL GENERAL HEALTH HOSPITAL (not its real name) awoke quite suddenly to a painful reality: it needed to change. Probing the data, leaders had noticed worrisome performance trends, including more frequent patient and staff injuries, higher-than-average turnover in nursing staff, and declining patient experience scores that undermined the organization's brand. The organization had become siloed, with nurses, physicians, and clinical support services all occupying their own domains, and service line teams (formed to improve patient care) maintaining disparate reporting structures. Physicians, for example, worked in the hospital, but didn't answer to the hospital, and therefore lacked accountability to team members who did.

Letters from patients and family members underscored the organization's need to improve—and fast. As one employee wrote on an engagement survey: "It feels like Central General cares more about its awards than caring for its patients." As another echoed in a patient experience survey: "I have complex chronic conditions, and you have all my specialists. It's the best place to get care, but no one can see me on the same day or coordinate with other clinics so that I can make one trip instead of five. Why can't someone help me coordinate my appointments?"

During the following few months, the hospital introduced new processes and systems to deliver excellent care, drawing on a collaboration among pharmacy, biomedical engineering, and information technology (IT) departments to optimize unit design, create easier lines of sight from the nurses' station, and redesign patient rooms. Leaders also aligned the organization around a definition of quality that centered on the patient and caregiver experience, and agreed on an improvement plan. Reaching across the silos, they collaborated with caregivers, patients, and families to arrive at specific solutions that improved safety, patient experience, and caregiver engagement all at once. The hospital also overhauled its human resources onboarding and orientation to provide tools and resources people needed to care compassionately for patients. Leaders realized that they needed to commit to improvement over the long term, addressing problems in performance as they arose, and admitting to mistakes when they made them. As one leader said, "This was about transforming the culture and leveraging our people and improvement methodologies to help drive consistency across the growing system. That way, we'd ensure this was not only the best place to receive care, but the best place to deliver it, study it, and advance it."

Across healthcare today, the traditional, siloed approach to improving care—in which one team focuses on initiatives to drive safety, another team focuses on initiatives to drive engagement, and a third works to improve efficiency—is proving inadequate. Even when siloed organizations do manage performance gains, they're usually slow and difficult to sustain. Organizations must bring people together if they are to truly transform themselves, mobilizing cross-functional teams to define and communicate strategic imperatives and to execute on the operational plan. Drawing on our experience helping hundreds of health systems and medical groups pursue cultural transformations, we'll present six key Transformational Principles™ [1] that the most successful organizations, like Central General Health, use to revitalize their cultures and drive performance (Figure 11.1). We'll also discuss how top organizations execute transformation plans to best ensure improvements in patient experience.

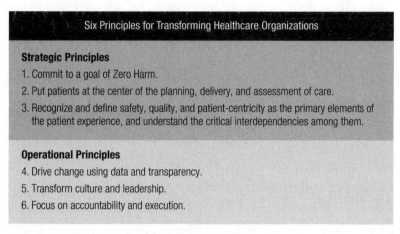

Six Principles for Transforming Healthcare Organizations

Strategic Principles
1. Commit to a goal of Zero Harm.
2. Put patients at the center of the planning, delivery, and assessment of care.
3. Recognize and define safety, quality, and patient-centricity as the primary elements of the patient experience, and understand the critical interdependencies among them.

Operational Principles
4. Drive change using data and transparency.
5. Transform culture and leadership.
6. Focus on accountability and execution.

Figure 11.1   Six Key Transformational Principles

You might well wonder why organizations need a framework of principles guiding their transformation. It's simple: idea overload. In their drive to increase the value of the care they deliver and to lower costs in the face of ever more rapid change, leaders feel overwhelmed and are unsure which improvement efforts to prioritize. Organizations become overwhelmed, too. Most have large portfolios of goals but limited money and staff with which to execute. Caregivers lack clarity about the strategy and its relation to their work, and they wonder whether leaders will remain focused on that strategy for very long. In addition, executional failures demoralize staff and paralyze an organization's ability to improve performance, as tantalizing as many visions of the future might be.

To break free of idea overload, let's take a step back. Despite the manifold changes in healthcare, its core building blocks remain the same: highly engaged and talented people delivering safe, high-quality, and compassionate care experiences. No matter how impressive the technology, architecture, or amenities, what sets excellent organizations apart is their ability to consistently deliver exceptional experiences. Safety matters. Clinical quality and operational efficiencies matter. Compassion and empathy matter. Seamless collaboration matters. Somehow, caregivers must unite and do their very best when patients and families need them most. Leaders who remain mindful of this singular purpose and allow it to suffuse decision-making can boost engagement and unlock their workforce's full potential as caregivers.

Yet leaders need something else: a comprehensive framework to simplify and help organize their efforts. A well-conceived framework lends transformation strategic importance inside organizations, providing much-needed clarity about direction, tasks, and expectations. To accelerate change, improvement, and ultimately transformation, we must structure our thinking in ways that break down siloed approaches and embrace holistic thinking. Our six principles for transformation do exactly that. They fall into two categories, each containing three components. The first three principles are strategic, setting the course for how to align the organization and create boundaries. The second three are more tactical and operational.

Strategic Principles

When undertaking any transformation, an organization must return to the basics and focus on why employees and leaders chose healthcare as a profession: to care for patients. Given this purpose's centrality, we must renew the organization's commitment to healing and comforting, beginning by speaking honestly about the patient experience. High-performing organizations define patient experience broadly as encompassing safe, high-quality, patient-centered care. That's a good start, but they must also embrace *a commitment to "Zero Harm."* By declaring such a noble goal, organizations can set their True North and embrace narratives, tools, and techniques to realize that goal. On the journey to Zero Harm, caregivers must begin by tracking serious safety events and communicating about instances of preventable harm.

As discussed in Chapter 10, organizations must also measure employee safety. Slips, trips, falls, strains, and needlesticks plague healthcare, and Zero Harm entails eradicating harm for patients and caregivers alike. Our research in safety and High Reliability through Healthcare Performance Improvement (HPI), a Press Ganey solution, shows that when organizations focus on measuring and reducing harm to patients, they experience as much as an 80 percent reduction in serious safety events.[2] Organizations shouldn't simply measure harm; they should also leverage proven practices to inspire a commitment to Zero Harm among the workforce. These practices include personalized storytelling, using patient and caregiver names and real-life experiences to "put a face" on safety.

When opening a large leadership meeting, a chief safety officer told of Mike Jones (not his real name), who was then in the ICU following a toxic medication overdose. Mr. Jones had questioned his care team about the medication they were set to administer him because it didn't resemble his previous dosage.

They reassured him it was accurate and administered it over his protests. The care team had not followed the safety checks and had given Mr. Jones medication intended for a different patient. The mistake didn't kill Mr. Jones, but it left him fighting for his life in the ICU. This story, with the patient's real name included, hit leaders at the meeting hard. "How could that happen here?" one leader asked. "We have such strict protocols and train consistently." By talking about real patients and staff, we elicit leaders' indignation, affirming that each event involves a human life and isn't reducible to a number. This first strategic element of transformation aligns caregivers and organizations around a cause that all find compelling.

In addition to committing to safety and the reduction of suffering, organizations must also embrace our second strategic principle: *putting patients and their families at the center of planning, delivery, and assessment of care.* True patient-centricity means adopting the best course of action and treatment for patients and families in all instances, not just when convenient for caregivers. Rather than just a placard on the wall, patient-centricity should encompass as many patient and family voices and preferences as possible. Organizations that prioritize patients include them as partners in codesigning systems, programs, and processes. They improve quickly because they've expanded the traditional view of the team to include people who interact with healthcare daily as patients, families, and ultimately consumers. As a strategic element of transformation, patient-centricity further connects caregivers to their work and drives engagement.

In its initial efforts to enhance clinical innovation and care delivery, Central General Health didn't adequately consider how patients, families, or caregivers experienced various processes and structures. As one leader was overheard saying at the time, "The focus was on clinical excellence and outcomes, but how it was delivered, achieved, or experienced wasn't given the same rigor or value." Leaders realized they had to expand their definition of "experience" to include clinical excellence, safety, efficiency, cost-effectiveness, and compassionate communication. This new formula truly put patients and families at the center of planning and execution. The organization continued to act on patient feedback gleaned from surveys, comments, and letters. Many patients and their families, they learned, wanted to help them "get it right" because they didn't want harm incidents to recur. This new perspective recast patients and families as problem-solvers and codesigners of change.

As eventual consumers ourselves, we in healthcare should all seek assurances that processes, systems, and people collaborate to drive successful experiences for patients and caregivers. This leads us to the third strategic principle: *the critical interdependencies of safety, quality, and patient-centricity*, all three of which define organizational experience. Leaders must advance their thinking, systems, and processes to cut across verticals and recognize interdependencies, creating a narrative to reinforce messaging consistently and effectively across the organization. Such a narrative requires full leadership engagement, and alignment with the organization's core values and expected behaviors. Forging meaningful narratives that are disseminated and understood at all levels of the organization requires time, patience, and strong communication plans.

Operational Principles

For organizations to drive transformation, they must pair a compelling narrative with a cohesive data strategy. That's why the fourth principle, and the first of our operational principles, entails *using data and transparency to drive change*. As we have seen throughout this book, data alone are not a strategy, and excessive data collection without action leads to "inaction fatigue." To use data strategically, organizations must first define data collection processes and key performance indicators (KPIs) to measure progress and commitment. These metrics should reflect areas of strength and opportunity and guide the organization toward consistently high performance. Metrics should also align with key strategic initiatives, displayed and monitored on board-level scorecards. Whereas organizations have traditionally considered safety, efficiency, and patient experience metrics in isolation from one another, leaders should now integrate these metrics to glean deeper insights. Doing so will allow them to maximize the (often) limited resources they have to effect change.

Central General Health integrated metrics during its transformational journey, expanding the types of information its CEO quality forums and board regularly reviewed. Traditionally focused on clinical outcomes, pathways, and the success rates of clinical interventions alone, leaders enhanced their understanding of quality by also reviewing indicators like teamwork, patient experience measures, and employee and provider engagement. At all organizations, leaders must also review KPIs among themselves and with frontline caregivers, because sharing such data transparently further erodes silos and reinforces the interdependencies of safety, quality, experience, and engagement.

As the chapters in this book collectively argue, culture can help expand these interdependencies, which is why organizations on a transformational journey must prioritize it. To that end, our fifth principle is to *transform organizational cultures and focus on developing leaders and high-performing teams.* Leaders can begin by implementing the culture-shaping principles of Zero Harm and patient-centricity described previously. We must also commit to eradicating workforce cancers like bullying and incivility, discussed in Chapter 9. High-performing teams in which colleagues work together toward common goals and hold one another accountable for standards of conduct will cement the culture required for transformational change.

Legendary UCLA basketball coach John Wooden once commented that, "You can't have a good (basketball) team without good players, you can't have good players without good skills, and you can't have good skills without good practice."[3] A similar principle applies in healthcare. The structure, sense of direction (strategy), and understanding of how we fit in all contribute to our success, as does our ability to practice and coordinate well with one another. But, unlike in basketball, we're operating in life-and-death situations. Teamwork matters most when an organization finds itself at the epicenter of a crisis, such as a mass shooting or natural disaster. Then, everyone must play a role, align with the overall strategy, and collaborate. Organizations that build such teamwork and solidarity continue to lead and lay the foundation for high performance in the future.

The sixth, and final, transformational principle is to *focus on accountability and execution*. Here, many initiatives fail. Guy Kawasaki of Apple Macintosh fame is rumored to have said that, "Ideas are easy. Implementation is hard."[4] Coach Wooden also reminded us to "never mistake activity for achievement."[5] In healthcare, we often find organizations concentrating most of their attention on planning rather than implementation. We must develop strategies to convert ideas to actions, and this final principle gives organizations the prodding to do just that. The most effective way to ensure that plans become actions is to institute a continuous improvement method, and to make initiatives part of caregivers' daily standard work. Implementing personal, peer, leader, and patient accountability measures can also ensure that initiatives persist over time.

As transformation proceeded at Central General, the organization's renewed clarity and purpose shaped interactions and the overall culture. All team members received updated descriptions and attended a four-hour workshop that refreshed everyone on the history and current landscape of healthcare and how their roles directly impact care delivery. The training simultaneously reinforced the mission and underscored the values and behavioral standards necessary to fulfill it across every discipline, department, and person at Central General. Although some employees and managers resisted change, a portion of them decided on their own to leave, while others were persuaded to commit to the new culture.

10 Steps for Sharpening Execution

When attempting to transform an organization, leaders must stay focused and persistent—they simply can't tolerate traditional ways of thinking and executing. A structured framework that includes the strategic and tactical elements described in this chapter establishes a stable foundation for transformation. But to achieve their goals, leaders must reassess the impact of strategic plans on an ongoing basis and modify them as necessary. Let's now consider 10 steps, derived from years of working with large health systems, for embarking on the path toward successful implementation. These steps form a checklist against which organizations can assess their current transformational efforts.

To execute well, leaders must ensure that patient experience, as defined previously, remains a strategic priority (**Step #1**). High levels of visibility and prioritization, including board-level reporting and resourcing, help reinforce the importance of patient experience, as does the sharing of patient and caregiver stories at the opening of meetings and huddles. At one organization we work with, the daily tiered huddle starts with an experience story to ground all participants in the organization's central purpose and how the day of work ahead connects to that purpose.

Leaders must also define a coherent *vision* of a desired patient experience and what it means for your organization (**Step #2**). Leaders must ask themselves: What does the organization intend to deliver for patients? What is the environment it wants to create for its caregivers? Press Ganey suggests that organizations think about a desired patient experience as "the consistent delivery of safe, high-quality, patient-centered care."

After defining the patient experience, leaders should create a common vocabulary—a "narrative"—that enables everyone to talk about patient experience in a common way (**Step #3**). The narrative should help define the "burning platform," explaining *why* this work matters to the organization and *how* all roles connect in the pursuit of excellence. The University of Tennessee Medical Center in Knoxville, Tennessee, defined its narrative by communicating three simple sentences to all team members: "Together Safe. Together Effective. Always for Our Patients." Leaders use this mantra frequently in daily conversations, succinctly capturing the organization's priorities for team members and giving them language they can reference in their own work.

To ensure that the organization helps build the vision and narrative, leaders should consider crowdsourcing. All employees, including physicians, should take part. When fully developed, the organization's narrative can serve as the basis for talent management and ongoing education across the organization. Several best practices can also bolster this work. Leaders should begin by leveraging the Patient and Family Advisory Council (PFAC) in defining elements of patient experience. They should next utilize town hall meetings and in-person sessions as well as the organization's internal communication methods to engage providers and staff, solicit feedback, and begin disseminating the definition and narrative. Test the definition with key leaders before rolling it out across the organization. It is also important to ensure that the organization's mission, vision, and values align with the narrative and performance expectations. Many organizations use visual maps or guides to facilitate dialogue and shared understanding, and to cascade and embed messaging throughout the organization.

High-performing organizations integrate the narrative of transformation into the *enterprise communication strategy*, often using internal communications or marketing teams (**Step #4**). Such teams should distinguish among external and internal branding and messaging. Internal efforts help align caregivers and leadership around the shared mission and provide progress updates, while external efforts seek to grow the business and engage with the community. In all instances, messaging should highlight patient-centered care and the organization's performance on key outcome metrics, allowing internal stakeholders to understand the links between patient and caregiver experience. Internal communication teams and their messaging play a vital role in ensuring all caregivers receive timely and meaningful work updates as well as recognition for their everyday efforts. As our data show, increasing communication also fosters a culture of engagement.

The communications team should partner with senior leaders to design the modes and frequency of messaging around the organization's patient experience efforts. Many teams find it initially helpful to determine the long-range messaging schedule and then work backward to determine details such as the authors, intended audience, and key points of each message. Doing so can help a team pin down a cadence and format for communication and elucidate the connection between each caregiver's unique role and the organization's desired direction. Increasing communication also helps employees become more familiar with leaders and better understand organizational news. A proper communications plan allows for a continuous feedback loop whereby caregivers can submit questions for inclusion in future communications.

The communications team should pay close attention to tone, time of day, and audience when framing communications, but they should also make sure that the plan contains mechanisms for sharing critical updates outside of the typical cadence. One organization we work with uses a standard quarterly leadership forum they call LDI (or Leadership Development Institute) to disseminate messages to leaders. During those meetings, all 3,000 leaders attend an educational event, gaining exposure to new skills and learning of events across the health system. Despite such efforts, the organization was surprised to learn of declining employee engagement numbers. The chief executive officer (CEO) and the chief human resources officer decided to publicize this diminished performance aggressively, and to promote a remediation plan. The organization now uses three- to four-minute-long videos of senior leaders to present frequent updates across the system. As their experience suggests, leaders should allow for a certain amount of flexibility in their communications efforts. Messaging that features data should also be clear, concise, and easy to understand. Establishing goals around mean score as opposed to percentile ranks (Chapter 5) is a clear and consistent way to engage front-line leaders in the goal-setting and improvement process. Once the decision has been made to set goals on a mean score, only communicating changes in performance around mean (and not muddying communications with additional metrics) provides the clarity leaders need to understand performance.

To accelerate improvement efforts, create a cross-functional team of multidisciplinary leaders to serve as an executive steering committee for patient experience (**Step #5**). This team should drive strategy and receive updates from intermediary committees and task forces responsible for key tactics and initiatives. High-performing organizations focus on how these teams work to drive patient experience efforts. Once the team is formed, for example, leaders should set a cadence for team meetings, and stick to it with a discipline rivaling that of clinical and financial steering committees. Leaders should create subcommittees representing services across the system (medicine, nursing, social work, pharmacy, facilities, environmental, IT, and so on). Allow these subcommittees to operate autonomously for set periods of time, reporting back to the executive steering committee on a regular basis with progress updates. Finally, leaders should define the hierarchy of governance with formal sponsors, establish chairs and charters for each subcommittee, and illustrate how they connect to the broader body of work.

Given this book's emphasis on measurement, readers can now appreciate how crucial data strategy is to execution. The next step is to adopt a dynamic data strategy (**Step #6**). As we've discussed, an organization must identify KPIs and include them on a balanced scorecard. A standard process for data collection and dissemination of findings should exist, including the use of leading, real-time, and lagging indicators of performance. Organizations should communicate transparently about performance at all levels to drive internal improvements as well as an external, consumer strategy. When possible, validated measurement tools should collect data, and leaders should leverage existing, enterprise-wide, High Reliability and/or continuous improvement methodologies to further create alignment. Finally, organizations should ensure that they map each goal to specific behaviors throughout the organization to measure performance, improvement, and sustainability in a comprehensive and specific way.

Defining organizational standards of behavior (as discussed in this book's Introduction and first chapter) in alignment with the True North (**Step #7**) is another best practice. If leaders, managers, and frontline caregivers alike agree on expectations and their purpose, accountability will follow in due course. If behavioral standards remain unmet, consider how better to roll them out, train for them, and reinforce them in the course of daily work. Chapter 1 outlined key aspects of strategic talent management and how it reinforces patient experience and transformation. **Step #8** involves integrating transformation efforts fully with strategic talent management, hiring, onboarding, and developing the talent needed to live key values, reinforce the narrative, and deliver on the patient promise of safe, high-quality, patient-centered care. Absent the right caregivers, execution will always pose a significant challenge for organizations.

Theo Epstein, the president of baseball operations of the Chicago Cubs, subscribed to a similar way of thinking. In 2017, *Fortune Magazine* named him the "World's Best Leader" based on his turnaround of the Cubs and their winning of the 2016 World Series. Epstein accepted the role of president of baseball operations in 2012, when he promised the city of Chicago a World Series under his leadership (no small promise, considering the Cubs hadn't achieved this goal since 1908). Epstein set out to build a high-performing team by focusing on character, discipline, and chemistry, three characteristics that he felt were essential to turning "skilled athletes into leaders."[6]

To test for these attributes, Cubs' scouts asked all players for examples of how they overcame adversity on the field and in their personal lives. Scouts analyzed these answers to understand how a given player would fit within the Cubs' system. No matter how talented a player was, the absence of a cultural fit meant no contract. Healthcare would do well to adopt this same approach. What if every recruiter asked nurse candidates about how they overcame adversity in their personal lives and at the bedside? Wouldn't this provide insight into the nurse's potential cultural fit? By rethinking how we assess talent, we ensure that we're attracting, recruiting, and onboarding caregivers who align with the organization's larger goals and mission. No matter how technically skilled a caregiver might be, the absence of a cultural fit should also mean no contract. Ultimately, Epstein credited the relentless pursuit of these three personal attributes for the team's World Series victory.

Step #9 is to make the transformation provider-centric. Accelerating transformation requires strong physician under-standing and support, so you need a strategy for engaging medical staff, advanced practice providers, and faculty. Organizations can leverage several high-value tactics, including identification of a well-known physician to lead the effort; establishment of a physician task force that includes formal leaders, informal leaders, and potential detractors; and engagement with detractors to help "turn them around" and generate buy-in. When including "naysayers," present a case for "what's in it for them" to join the team. Once your team is in place, empower the task force to tackle the following three tasks: defining the physician's role in patient experience, developing a physician narrative that describes "how physician leaders should talk about the patient experience," and develop-ing educational materials that the organization can distribute to medical staff. These tasks often go unprioritized due to myriad demands on physicians, but you neglect them at your peril.

The final step (**Step #10**) is to focus tactics and best practices with an eye toward simplification. When everything is a prior-ity, nothing ultimately is. To that end, take an inventory of your existing practices across the four domains of patient experience, including enterprise and unit-based activities such as huddles, rounding, and communication mediums. High-performing orga-nizations measure the effectiveness of each and compare policies and procedures across different locations to understand incon-sistencies in practice. This analysis helps align each initiative to the patient experience, and it allows organizations to determine areas of convergence and opportunities for streamlining tools and methods. Remove activities that don't meet objectives or are inef-fective or outdated. We saw Hawaii Pacific's Get Rid of Stupid Stuff (GROSS) Program do this in Chapter 9. When necessary, introduce best practices such as executive, leadership, and man-ager rounds; purposeful hourly nursing rounds; bedside shift reports; whiteboards; physician communication training; and service recovery training. Delivered consistently, these tactics can effect change across the continuum.

Conclusion

Launched on a quest for excellence, leaders at Central General Health have used the framework in this chapter to continuously reassess their strategy and the operational support required to deliver on it. Harnessing the talent and unwavering commitment of their people, they've connected strategy and purpose with daily operations, improving critical outcomes for patients and families. Such efforts took time, but as the organization's CEO told us, they unlocked unprecedented levels of performance. "Through our commitment to listen, include others on the care team, and innovate new solutions, we've not only returned to delivering on the basics, we've been able to accelerate our success," he said. "We took the time to strengthen our foundation, invest in our employees, and create the type of environment and culture that allows people to again believe that we are the best place for care to be delivered, invented, and received."

Achieving high performance and cultivating a spirit of continuous improvement doesn't happen overnight. Even with the powerful framework and recommendations described in this chapter, most organizations take five to seven years to complete their transformational journey. Remain diligent, even during the tough times. It's the only way to change care delivery in meaningful ways, and in the process to create a passionate and fully engaged workforce.

IN SUM

- To unlock their potential, organizations must formulate a cohesive and integrated strategy aimed at driving safe, high-quality, patient-centered care.
- Such a strategy must arise out of a commitment to Zero Harm, patient-centricity, and the interdependencies of safety, quality, patient experience, and employee engagement.
- Although execution is an ongoing challenge, certain proven tactics can help an organization drive and sustain improvement over time.
- Transformation takes time. Stay the course to maximize your chances of success.

Notes

Introduction

1. For privacy reasons, we have altered significant details of this story.
2. Material taken from unpublished Press Ganey workforce engagement data.
3. "Achieving Excellence: The Convergence of Safety, Quality, Experience and Caregiver Engagement," *2017 Strategic Insights Report* (white paper, Press Ganey, 2017), 5.
4. "Achieving Excellence: The Convergence of Safety, Quality, Experience and Caregiver Engagement," 8.
5. Reporting on a survey conducted in February 2019, JP Morgan observed that, "US healthcare organizations are wrestling with a challenging duality . . . while the majority expect to increase hiring for physicians and nurses, there may not be enough talent to meet their needs, as 58% of respondents said they are extremely or very concerned about finding candidates with the right skill set." Beth Jones Sanborn, "Talent Shortage Is Plaguing Majority of Healthcare Execs, According to JP Morgan Survey," *Healthcare Finance*, accessed July 21, 2019, https://www.healthcarefinancenews.com/news/talent-shortage-plaguing-majority-healthcare-execs-according-jp-morgan-survey.
6. "Performance Insights: Resilience for a Multigenerational Nursing Workforce" (white paper, Press Ganey, October 23, 2018).
7. Maria Panagioti et al., "Association Between Physician Burnout and Patient Safety, Professionalism, and Patient Satisfaction: A Systematic Review and Meta-analysis," *JAMA Internal Medicine* (September 4, 2018), doi:10.1001/jamainternmed.2018.3713.
8. Troy Parks, "Report Reveals Severity of Burnout by Specialty," *American Medical Association*, January 31, 2017, https://www.ama-assn.org/practice-management/physician-health/report-reveals-severity-burnout-specialty.
9. Michael Dowling, "CEOs—Give a Damn About Your People," *Becker's Hospital Review*, April 26, 2019, https://www.beckershospitalreview.com/hospital-management-administration/michael-dowling-ceos-give-a-damn-about-your-people.html.

10. James Merlino, *Service Fanatics: How to Build Superior Patient Experience the Cleveland Clinic Way* (New York: McGraw-Hill, 2015), 15.
11. Derek Thompson, "Health Care Just Became the U.S.'s Largest Employer," *Atlantic*, January 9, 2018. https://www.theatlantic.com/business/archive/2018/01/health-care-america-jobs/550079/.

Chapter 1

1. Ben E. Dowell and Rob Silzer, *Strategy-Driven Talent Management: A Leadership Imperative* (San Francisco: Jossey-Bass, 2009), 18.
2. Ed Michaels, Helen Handfield-Jones, and Beth Axelrod, *The War for Talent* (Boston: Harvard Business School Press, 2001).
3. "Every Voice Matters: The Bottom Line on Employee and Physician Engagement" (white paper, Press Ganey, 2013).
4. Carol S. Dweck, *Mindset: The New Psychology of Success* (New York: Random House, 2016).
5. Minoo Javanmardian and Aditya Lingampally, "Can AI Address Health Care's Red-Tape Problem?" *Harvard Business Review*, November 5, 2018, https://hbr.org/2018/11/can-ai-address-health-cares-red-tape-problem.
6. Chris Schrader, Helen Leis, and Matthew Stevenson, "Defining Healthcare's Workforce for the Future. Shifting Demand Will Change the Nature of Work in Healthcare," *Oliver Wyman Health Innovation Journal*, 2 (December 2018).
7. Roy Maurer, "Closing the Looming Health Care Talent Gap: Can HR Find the Cure for What Ails US Health Care Systems?" *Society for Human Resource Management*, October 23, 2017, https://www.shrm.org/hr-today/news/hr-magazine/1117/pages/closing-the-looming-health-care-talent-gap.aspx.
8. Jason Narlock, "High Job Growth Expected for US Healthcare—But Where Will the Workers Be?" *Mercer*, November 16, 2017, https://www.mercer.com/our-thinking/career/voice-on-talent/high-job-growth-expected-for-us-healthcare-but-where-will-the-workers-be.html.
9. Joseph Cabral and Thomas H. Lee, "The New Healthcare CHRO: From Culture Keeper to Culture Driver," *Patient Safety & Quality Healthcare* (October 5, 2018), https://www.psqh.com/analysis/the-new-healthcare-chro-from-culture-keeper-to-culture-driver/.
10. Robert D. Putnam, *Bowling Alone: The Collapse and Revival of American Community* (New York: Simon & Schuster, 2000).
11. Jeff Schwartz et al., "The Future Is Here: The Future of Work," *Deloitte* (2018): 3, https://www2.deloitte.com/content/dam/Deloitte/us/Documents/life-sciences-health-care/us-lshc-future-of-work-health-care.pdf.
12. Peter W. Hom, "An exploratory investigation into theoretical mechanisms underlying realistic job previews," *Personnel Psychology* 51, vol. 2 (1998), http://dx.doi.org/10.1111/j.1744-6570.1998.tb00732.x.

13. Ernest O'Boyle, Jr., and Herman Aguinis, "The Best and the Rest: Revisiting the Norm of Normality in Individual Performance," *Personnel Psychology* 65, no. 1 (Spring 2012): 79–119.

14. "Humans Wanted," *Royal Bank of Canada*, 2018, https://www.rbc.com /dms/enterprise/futurelaunch/_assets-custom/pdf/RBC-Future-Skills -Report-FINAL-Singles.pdf.

15. Data compiled from Press Ganey's Sarah McLaughlin.

16. "2015 State of Engagement" (report, Press Ganey, May 2015).

17. Heather Boushey and Sarah Jane Glynn, "There Are Significant Business Costs to Replacing Employees" (report, Center for American Progress, November 16, 2012), https://www.americanprogress.org/issues/economy /reports/2012/11/16/44464/there-are-significant-business-costs-to -replacing-employees/.

18. Megan Wells, "Healthcare Turnover Rates in 2018," *Daily Pay*, November 14, 2018, https://business.dailypay.com/blog/employee-turnover-rates-in -the-healthcare-industry.

19. Jenna Filipkowski, "Talent Pulse," *Human Capital Institute*, June 2016: 4.

20. "Optimizing the Nursing Workforce: Key Drivers of Intent to Stay for Newly Licensed and Experienced Nurses" (report, Press Ganey, 2018), 1.

21. Russell Ray, "Who Will Replace Nuclear Power's Aging Work Force?" *Power Engineering,* February 5, 2015, https://www.power-eng.com/articles /npi/print/volume-8/issue-1/nucleus/who-will-replace-nuclear-power -s-aging-work-force.html.

22. Thomas F. Mahan, Danny Nelms, and Christopher Ryan Bearden, "2018 Retention Report: Truths and Trends in Turnover," *Work Institute Special Report*, 2018.

23. "Every Voice Matters: The Bottom Line on Employee and Physician Engagement" (report, Press Ganey, 2013).

24. Rachel Lefkowitz et al., "2018 Workplace Learning Report: The Rise and Responsibility of Talent Development in the New Labor Market" (LinkedIn Learning, 2018), 8.

25. Matt O'Brien, "Unemployment Is at a 50-Year Low, and It Might Drop a Lot Further," *Washington Post*, May 3, 2019, https://www.washingtonpost .com/business/2019/05/03/unemployment-is-year-low-it-might-drop-lot -further/?utm_term=.bbe8f3db60ca.

Chapter 2

1. Janice Hopkins Tanne, "Patients Are More Satisfied with Care from Doctors of Same Race," *British Medical Journal* 325, no. 7372 (November 9, 2002), https://www.ncbi.nlm.nih.gov/pmc/articles/PMC1124573/.

2. Marilyn Loden and Judy Rosener, *Workforce America! Managing Employee Diversity as a Vital Resource* (New York: Irwin, 1991), 17–20; 33.

3. "About Vernā Myers," *Vernā Myers Company*, accessed July 17, 2019, https://learning.vernamyers.com/pages/about-vern-myers.

4. Laura Sherbin and Ripa Rashid, "Diversity Doesn't Stick Without Inclusion," *Harvard Business Review*, February 1, 2017, https://hbr.org /2017/02/diversity-doesnt-stick-without-inclusion.

5. "Equal Employment Opportunity," *US Office of Personnel Management*, accessed July 22, 2019, https://www.opm.gov/equal-employment -opportunity/.

6. This is a written description of a graphic. Please see: "Illustrating Equality VS Equity," *Interaction Institute for Social Change*, January 13, 2016, https:// interactioninstitute.org/illustrating-equality-vs-equity/.

7. Tim Hume, "Young brothers, 'denied refuge,' swept to death by Sandy," *CNN*, November 4, 2012, https://www.cnn.com/2012/11/02/world /americas/sandy-staten-island-brothers/index.html.

8. "Implicit bias in health care," *Joint Commission* 23, April 2016, https://www .jointcommission.org/assets/1/23/Quick_Safety_Issue_23_Apr_2016.pdf.

9. *Merriam-Webster*, s.v., "microaggression," accessed July 22, 2019, https:// www.merriam-webster.com/dictionary/microaggression.

10. "About Diversity & Inclusion," *Cleveland Clinic*, accessed July 12, 2019, https://my.clevelandclinic.org/about/community/diversity/about.

Chapter 3

1. Tammy Wright (senior director, Voice of the Customer), "Novant Health: Integrating a Comprehensive Workforce and Engagement Strategy" (paper presented at Press Ganey National Client and Executive Leadership Conferences, Orlando, FL, November 2018).

2. Tammy Wright (senior director, Voice of the Customer), interview by author, June 12, 2019.

3. Pamela Hardy (Novant Health vice president of Learning and Development), interview by author, June 12, 2019.

Chapter 4

1. Daniel Goleman, Richard Boyatzis, and Annie McKee, *Primal Leadership: Realizing the Power of Emotional Intelligence* (Boston: Harvard Business Review Press, 2002), 6.

2. Kim Scott, *Radical Candor* (New York: St. Martin's Press, 2017).

3. Elaine Biech, *The Art and Science of Training* (Association for Talent Development Press, 2017), 23–25.

Chapter 5

1. Andrew Mercer, Claudia Deane, and Kyley Mcgeeney, "Why 2016 Election Polls Missed Their Mark," *Pew Research Center*, November 9, 2016, https://www.pewresearch.org/fact-tank/2016/11/09/why-2016-election-polls-missed-their-mark/.

2. "Why Press Ganey Surveys Are Valid" (Press Ganey, 2019).

3. D. J. Bartholomew, *Latent Variable Models and Factor Analysis* (New York: Oxford University Press, 1987), 2.

4. R. F. DeVellis, "Scale Development: Theory and Applications," *Scale Development: Theory and Applications*, Applied Social Research Methods Series, Vol. 26. (Thousand Oaks, CA: Sage Publications, Inc., 1991); "Calculating Section Scores and Overall Scores: The How and Why (R&A)" (Press Ganey, 2010).

5. "How to Drive an Engagement Strategy" (white paper, Press Ganey, November 2017).

6. "Achieving Excellence: The Convergence of Safety, Quality, Experience and Caregiver Engagement" (Press Ganey, March 2017), 8–14.

7. "Accelerating Transformation: Translating Strategy into Action" (Press Ganey, March 2019), 9–10.

8. "Mean Score vs. Percent Favorable" (Press Ganey, 2019).

9. "How to Drive an Engagement Strategy" (white paper, Press Ganey, November 2017).

10. "Driving Organizational Transformation: Metrics and Incentives" (white paper, Press Ganey, August 2018), 5–6.

Chapter 6

1. Aggregate metrics such as engagement, safety, and culture are well-suited for balanced scorecards at the organizational level, since they tend to broadly represent the organization's current state, tying well into quality measures, patient experience, and financial performance.

2. Karl E. Weick and Kathleen M. Sutcliffe, *Managing the Unexpected: Sustained Performance in a Complex World* (Hoboken, NJ: John Wiley & Sons, 2015), 8, 62 *et passim*.

3. Timothy J. Creasey and Robert Stise, eds., *Best Practices in Change Management 2016: 1120 Organizations Share Lessons and Best Practices in Change Management* (Prosci Incorporated, 2016), 19, 195.

Chapter 7

1. Christina Dempsey and Barbara A. Reilly, "Nurse Engagement: What Are the Contributing Factors for Success?" *Online Journal of Issues in Nursing* 21 (January 2016), doi: 10.3912/OJIN.Vol21No01Man02; K. Ostermeier and

K. M. Camp, "An Exploratory Investigation of Negative Perceptions of the Affordable Care Act Among Patient-Facing Professionals and Intentions to Leave," *Journal of Applied Management and Entrepreneurship* (2016), doi: http://dx.doi.org/10.9774/GLEAF.3709.2016.ap.00007.

2. Claire C. Caruso, "Negative Impacts of Shiftwork and Long Work Hours," *Rehabilitation Nursing Journal* 39 (January–February 2014): 16–25, doi: 10.1002/rnj.107.

3. Erick Messias et al., "Differences in Burnout Prevalence Between Clinical Professionals and Biomedical Scientists in an Academic Medical Centre: A Cross-Sectional Survey," *BMJ Open Journal* 9 (2019), 3, doi: 10.1136/bmjopen-2018-023506.

4. Ioanna V. Papathanasiou, "Work-Related Mental Consequences: Implications of Burnout on Mental Health Status Among Health Care Providers," *Acta Informatica Medica* 23 (February 2015): 23, doi: 10.5455/aim.2015.23.22–28.

5. Jeannie P. Cimiotti et al., "Nurse Staffing, Burnout, and Health Care–Associated Infection," *American Journal of Infection Control* 40, no. 6 (August 2012): 486–490, doi: 10.1016/j.ajic.2012.02.029.

6. Heather Spence Laschinger and Michael P. Leiter, "The Impact of Nursing Work Environments on Patient Safety Outcomes: The Mediating Role of Burnout/Engagement," *Journal of Nursing Administration* 36, no. 5 (May 2006): 265.

7. Amy Witkoski Stimpfel, Douglas M. Sloane, and Linda H. Aiken, "The Longer the Shifts for Hospital Nurses, the Higher the Levels of Burnout and Patient Dissatisfaction," *Health Affairs* 31, no. 11 (November 2012): 2501–9, doi:10.1377/hlthaff.2011.1377.

8. Linda H. Aiken et al., "Hospital Nurse Staffing and Patient Mortality, Nurse Burnout, and Job Dissatisfaction," *Journal of the American Medical Association* 288 (2002): 1987–1993, doi:10.1001/jama.288.16.1987.

9. "2019 National Health Care Retention & RN Staffing Report," *NSI Nursing Solutions, Inc.*, 2019, http://www.nsinursingsolutions.com/Files/assets/library/retention-institute/2019%20National%20Health%20Care%20Retention%20Report.pdf. 13_EM.docx.

10. "The Influence of Nurse Work Environment on Patient, Payment and Nurse Outcomes in Acute Care Settings" (report, Press Ganey, 2015).

11. "The Role of Workplace Safety and Surveillance Capacity in Driving Nurse and Patient Outcomes" (report, Press Ganey, 2016).

12. "The Influence of Nurse Manager Leadership on Patient and Nurse Outcomes and the Mediating Effects of the Nurse Work Environment" (report, Press Ganey, 2017).

13. Whitney McKnight, "Press Ganey CNO Roundtable: Developing and Supporting Nurse Managers" (Press Ganey, May 2017).

14. "Optimizing the Nursing Workforce: Key Drivers of Intent to Stay for Newly Licensed and Experienced Nurses" (report, Press Ganey, 2018).

15. Sherrie Bourg Carter, "The Tell Tale Signs of Burnout . . . Do You Have Them?" *Psychology Today*, November 26, 2013, https://www .psychologytoday.com/us/blog/high-octane-women/201311/the-tell-tale -signs-burnout-do-you-have-them.

16. "Kronos Survey Finds That Nurses Love What They Do Though Fatigue Is a Pervasive Problem," *Kronos*, May 8, 2017, https://www.kronos.com/about -us/newsroom/kronos-survey-finds-nurses-love-what-they-do-though -fatigue-pervasive-problem.

17. Lusine Poghosyan et al., "Nurse Burnout and Quality of Care: Cross-national Investigation in Six Countries," *Research in Nursing & Health* 33 (June 1, 2010): 8, doi: 10.1002/nur.20383.

18. "Burnout and Resilience: A Framework for Data Analysis and a Positive Path Forward" (white paper, Press Ganey, 2018).

19. "Burnout and Resilience: A Framework for Data Analysis and a Positive Path Forward" (white paper, Press Ganey, 2018).

20. "Resilience for a Multigenerational Workforce" (white paper, Press Ganey, 2018).

21. "Resilience for a Multigenerational Workforce" (white paper, Press Ganey, 2018).

22. Julie Kennedy Oehlert (chief experience officer for Vidant Health), interview by author (Christy Dempsey), July 16, 2019.

23. Christy Dempsey and Deirdre Mylod, "Addressing Patient and Caregiver Suffering," *American Nurse Today* 11, no. 11 (November 2016), https:// www.americannursetoday.com/addressing-patient-caregiver-suffering/.

Chapter 8

1. Dr. Anne Pendo (senior medical director for physician engagement at Intermountain Healthcare), interview by author (Chrissy Daniels), June 7, 2019.

2. Colin West et al., "Interventions to Prevent and Reduce Burnout: A Systematic Review and Meta-analysis," *Lancet* (November 2016), doi: 10.1016/S0140-6736(16)31279-X.

3. "2017 Survey of Final-Year Medical Residents: A Survey Examining the Career Preferences, Plans and Expectations of Physicians Completing Their Residency Training" (Merritt Hawkins, 2017):12, https://www .merritthawkins.com/uploadedFiles/mha_2017_resident_survey.pdf; "A Unified Approach to Drive Patient and Physician Loyalty" (Press Ganey, June 6, 2019).

4. "Medscape National Physician Compensation Report 2018" (Medscape, 2018).

5. Shasha Han et al., "Estimating the Attributable Cost of Physician Burnout in the United States," *Annals of Internal Medicine* 170, no. 11 (2019), doi: 10.7326/M18-1422 2019.

6. "National Physician Burnout, Depression & Suicide Report," *Medscape*, January 16, 2019, https://www.medscape.com/slideshow/2019-lifestyle -burnout-depression-6011056#5.

7. "A Unified Approach to Drive Patient and Physician Loyalty" (Press Ganey, June 6, 2019), 8.

8. "The Complexities of Physician Supply and Demand: Projections from 2017 to 2032," *Association of Medical Colleges*, April 2019, viii, https://aamc -black.global.ssl.fastly.net/production/media/filer_public/31/13/3113ee5c -a038-4c16-89af-294a69826650/2019_update_-_the_complexities_of _physician_supply_and_demand_-_projections_from_2017-2032.pdf.

9. Linda T. Kohn, Janet Corrigan, and Molla S. Donaldson, eds. *To Err Is Human: Building a Safer Health System* (Washington, D.C.: National Academy Press, 2000).

10. Marc Harrison, "How a US Health Care System Uses 15-Minute Huddles to Keep a 23-Hospital System Aligned," *Harvard Business Review*, November 29, 2018, https://hbr.org/2018/11/how-a-u-s-health-care -system-uses-15-minute-huddles-to-keep-23-hospitals-aligned.

11. Dr. Virginia Casey and Jennifer L. Schenk, "Building a Culture of Wellness in an Orthopedic Group" (paper presented at Pediatric Orthopedic Society of North America, July 2019).

12. Dr. Virginia Casey (chief medical officer of OrthoCarolina), interview by author (Matt Turner), 2019.

13. Material taken from the Press Ganey national database and research.

14. "Physician Leadership Institute," *Institute for Healthcare Improvement*, accessed July 22, 2019, http://app.ihi.org/FacultyDocuments/Events /Event-2930/Presentation-15534/Document-12586/Tools_Resource_Q7 _PLI_Handout.pdf.

15. Carl S. Armato and Tom E. Jenike, "Physician Resiliency and Wellness for Transforming a Health System," *NEJM Catalyst*, May 2, 2018, https:// catalyst.nejm.org/leadership-development-program-physician-resiliency -wellness/.

16. Ralph Yates (Salem Health's chief medical officer), interview by author (Chrissy Daniels), July 2019.

Chapter 9

1. "Burn-out an 'Occupational Phenomenon': International Classification of Diseases," *World Health Organization*, May 28, 2019, https://www.who.int /mental_health/evidence/burn-out/en/.

2. Christina Maslach, Susan E. Jackson, and Michael P. Leiter, "Overview of the Maslach Burnout Inventory," in *Maslach Burnout Inventory: Manual 4th Edition* (Mind Garden, 2018), 1–12.

3. M. Tugade and B. Fredrickson, "Resilient Individuals Use Emotions to Bounce Back from Negative Emotional Experiences," *Journal of Personality and Social Psychology* 86, no. 2 (2004): 320–333.

4. *Through the Eyes of the Workforce: Creating Joy, Meaning and Safer Health Care* (Boston: National Patient Safety Foundation, 2013), 1–2.

5. Tait D. Shanafelt and John H. Noseworthy, "Executive Leadership and Physician Well-being," *Mayo Clinic Proceedings* 92 (January 2017): 129–146, http://dx.doi.org/10.1016/j.mayocp.2016.10.004.

6. Tait D. Shanafelt et al., "Career Fit and Burnout Among Academic Faculty," *Archives of Internal Medicine* 169 (2009): 990–995, doi: 10.1001/archinternmed.2009.70.

7. Deirdre E. Mylod, "One Way to Prevent Clinician Burnout," *Harvard Business Review,* October 23, 2017, https://hbr.org/2017/10/one-way-to-prevent-clinician-burnout.

8. "Medscape National Physician Burnout & Depression Report 2018," *Medscape,* January 17, 2018, https://www.medscape.com/slideshow/2019-lifestyle-burnout-depression-6011056.

9. "Healthy Nurse Healthy Nation™ Year One Highlights," *American Nurse Today,* January 28, 2019, https://www.americannursetoday.com/hnhn-year-one-highlights/.

10. Deirdre E. Mylod and Thomas H. Lee, "Helping Health Care Workers Avoid Burnout," *Harvard Business Review,* October 12, 2018, https://hbr.org/2018/10/helping-health-care-workers-avoid-burnout.

11. Christine A. Sinsky, "In Search of Joy in Practice: A Report of 23 High-Functioning Primary Care Practices," *Annals of Family Medicine* 11, no. 3 (2013): 272–78, doi:10.1370/afm.1531.

12. Melinda Ashton, "Getting Rid of Stupid Stuff," *New England Journal of Medicine* 379, no. 19 (2018): 1789–1791, doi:10.1056/nejmp1809698.

13. "Founding Executive Council Insights—Clinician Burnout: Amplifying Rewards and Mitigating Stress," *Institute for Innovation,* August 13, 2018, http://www.theinstituteforinnovation.org/docs/default-source/findings/clinician-burnout_amplifying-rewards-and-mitigating-stress_draft_v3.pdf?sfvrsn=2.

14. Molly Gamble, "Why Mayo Clinic Is Picking up the Check for Physicians to Dine Together," *Becker's Hospital Review,* May 3, 2016, https://www.beckershospitalreview.com/hospital-physician-relationships/why-mayo-clinic-is-picking-up-the-check-for-physicians-to-dine-together.html.

15. "Founding Executive Council Insights—Clinician Burnout: Amplifying Rewards and Mitigating Stress," *Institute for Innovation,* August 13, 2018, http://www.theinstituteforinnovation.org/docs/default-source/findings/clinician-burnout_amplifying-rewards-and-mitigating-stress_draft_v3.pdf?sfvrsn=2.

16. "Healthy Nurse Healthy Nation™ Year One Highlights," *American Nurse Today*, January 28, 2019, https://www.americannursetoday.com/hnhn-year-one-highlights/.

Chapter 10

1. *To Err Is Human: Building a Safer Health System* (Washington, D.C.: National Academy Press, 2000), 26, https://doi.org/10.17226/9728.
2. Scott Harris, "Safety Culture in Healthcare: The $13 billion case," *Safety Management* (October 2013), 49, 54.
3. Drs. Rich Brilli and Terry Davis (Nationwide Children's Hospital), interview by authors, June 18, 2019.
4. Charles Duhigg, *The Power of Habit* (New York: Random House, 2012), 98–100.
5. Dr. Christopher Trotz (executive medical director for the 150 locations of Inspira Medical Group), interview by authors, June 25, 2019.

Chapter 11

1. "A Strategic Blueprint for Transformational Change," Press Ganey, April 2018, 9.
2. Craig Clapper, James Merlino, and Carole Stockmeier, *Zero Harm: How to Achieve Patient and Workforce Safety in Healthcare* (New York: McGraw-Hill, 2018), 5.
3. John Wooden and Don Yaeger, *A Game Plan for Life: The Power of Mentoring* (New York: Bloomsbury: 2009), 40.
4. Craig Impelman, "Never Mistake Activity for Achievement," *Wooden Effect*, June 20, 2018, https://www.thewoodeneffect.com/activity-achievement/.
5. John Wooden and Jay Carty, *Coach Wooden's Pyramid of Success: Building Blocks for a Better Life* (Ada, MI: Revell, 2005).
6. Tom Verducci, "Why Theo Epstein and the Cubs Are Fortune's MVPs This Year," *Fortune*, March 23, 2017, http://fortune.com/2017/03/23/theo-epstein-chicago-cubs-worlds-greatest-leaders/.

Index

About the Authors

Mary Jo Assi, DNP, RN, NEA-BC, FAAN, is Press Ganey's Associate Chief Nursing Officer, leading strategies for strengthening caregiver resilience and engagement, reducing patient suffering, and delivering compassionate, connected care. Prior to joining Press Ganey, Mary Jo was vice president of nursing practice and innovation at the American Nurses Association (ANA). While serving in this capacity, she led the organization's strategic initiative to develop a Center of Innovation to promote and support best practices for enhancing the nursing work environment. Prior to this work, she led additional ANA initiatives focusing on quality care and patient and nurse health, wellness, and safety, including Healthy Nurse, Healthy Nation™; Scope and Standards of Nursing Practice; and Healthy Work Environment.

Mary Jo has published on a broad range of topics, including quality, safety, and nursing leadership, and has presented both nationally and internationally on topics ranging from nurse staffing to the application of data and research to the practice setting, enhancing the practice and work environment and caring for the caregiver. She is an adjunct professor at Florida Atlantic University where she teaches in the doctoral nursing program.

Rachel Biblow is the Senior Vice President of Transformational Solutions at Press Ganey. In her role, she provides strategic vision and partners with organizations to achieve transformational and sustainable improvements across safety, quality, experience, and engagement.

Rachel joined Press Ganey in 2018, bringing expertise in advancing safe, high-quality, compassionate care experiences and building highly engaged teams. Prior to joining Press Ganey, she served for more than 15 years at the Children's Hospital of Philadelphia, most recently as the senior director of Patient and Family Services and enterprise cosponsor for the Patient and Family Experience initiative. During her tenure, she worked directly with patients and families, as well as served in a variety of leadership roles with expanding scope and influence. In addition to the strategic and operational oversight for several clinical and clinical support areas, she led the design, strategy, and implementation of an enterprise-wide initiative to improve overall patient and family engagement and experience.

Rachel is widely recognized for her work in advancing patient and family partnerships with health systems to drive quality outcomes. She is a founding leader in establishing the National Pediatric Experience Collaborative formed in 2016. The Collaborative is a consortium of leading children's hospitals working together to improve and advance safe, high-quality, compassionate care experiences across all systems. She is an international speaker on experience, patient- and family-centered care, and social work leadership, and has presented at multiple health systems and conferences.

Craig Clapper, PE, CMQ/OE, is a founding partner of Healthcare Performance Improvement (HPI) and a Partner in Press Ganey Transformational Services. Press Ganey HPI is a consulting group that specializes in improving human performance in complex systems using evidence-based methods from High Reliability Organizations.

Craig has 30 years of experience improving reliability in nuclear power, transportation, manufacturing, and healthcare. He specializes in cause analysis, reliability improvement, and safety culture improvements. Craig has led safety culture transformation engagements for Duke Energy, the US Department of Energy, ABB, Westinghouse, Framatome ANP, and several healthcare systems.

Prior to joining Press Ganey, Craig was the chief knowledge officer of HPI, chief operating officer of HPI, chief operating officer of Performance Improvement International, systems engineering manager for Hope Creek Nuclear Generating Station, and systems engineering manager for Palo Verde Nuclear Generation Station. Craig holds a bachelor of science degree in nuclear engineering from Iowa State University, earned a professional engineer (PE) license, and is a certified manager of Quality and Organizational Excellence (CMQ/OE), American Society for Quality (ASQ).

Chrissy Daniels, MS, joined Press Ganey in August 2017, bringing to her role of Consulting Partner more than 20 years of expertise in advancing the patient experience and building an engaging and collaborative culture. She is also widely recognized for her pioneering work in the areas of consumerism and physician performance data transparency.

Prior to joining Press Ganey, Chrissy was director of strategic initiatives at University of Utah Health Care, responsible for teaching and coaching leaders, physicians, and staff on the importance of patient experience as a measure of quality. In this role, she was also responsible for designing the University of Utah Health Care's online physician review process, making the system the first in the country to electronically survey its patients and post the results publicly online. In addition, Chrissy worked closely with hospital, physician, and executive leadership to drive culture change around improving patient experience and value in every encounter across the system.

Christina Dempsey, DNP, MSN, CNOR, CENP, FAAN, is Press Ganey's Chief Nursing Officer, responsible for providing clinical guidance to help clients transform the patient experience. She leads the team in the organization's efforts to reduce patient suffering and develop compassionate and connected care across the continuum.

In her present role, as well as previously as leader of clinical and operational consulting services for Press Ganey, Christy has worked to improve employee and physician engagement, improve the flow of patients throughout organizations, improve quality and efficiency, and prepare organizations for healthcare reform. Christy is a registered nurse with over three decades of healthcare experience in nursing, perioperative and emergency services management, medical practice, supply chain and materials management, and physician–hospital collaboration.

Christy frequently speaks and publishes nationally and internationally on patient experience, nursing, patient flow, physician–hospital collaboration, and balancing cost and quality. In November 2017, she released her first book, *The Antidote to Suffering: How Compassionate Connected Care Can Improve Safety, Quality, and Experience*, published by McGraw-Hill. Christy holds a doctorate degree in nursing practice and master's degrees in both business and nursing, and is certified in perioperative nursing and executive nursing practice.

Lynn Ehrmantraut is the Senior Vice President of Engagement Services at Press Ganey. She provides direction for all aspects of the Engagement business unit and coordinates the execution of thought leadership. She directs the corporate strategic Engagement products and services road map, innovation, development, and launch to grow the division. Lynn collaborates with senior leaders on partnership and acquisition opportunities and across the company to support clients.

Lynn joined Press Ganey in 2016 as part of the Avatar Solutions acquisition where she served as senior vice president. Lynn has more than 30 years of experience in a variety of acute, behavioral, and post-acute healthcare settings, focused on employee engagement, strategic planning, performance improvement, customer service, informatics, and risk management. Prior organizations include Eisenhower Medical Center, The Betty Ford Center, and Quorum Health Resources.

Lynn holds a master of business administration degree from the University of Phoenix and an undergraduate degree in health information administration from the College of St. Scholastica. She is a registered health information administrator and certified quality professional through NAHQ's CPHQ certification program.

Eric W. Heckerson, EdD, RN, FACHE, joined Press Ganey in 2018 and is currently Senior Director of Organizational Development and Performance. In this role, Eric is responsible for assessing and developing internal leadership and talent, along with crafting and overseeing a strategy for engaging associates at all levels of the organization. He brings 25 years of experience in healthcare and organizational development as a registered nurse, healthcare leader, consultant, and educator.

Eric is passionate about blending learning, leadership, and strategy together to create practical and sustainable tactics for developing others professionally, improving the quality of the workplace, and making a difference in the lives of others. He has authored several academic articles, serves as university-based adjunct faculty, and lectures on leadership, learning, change management, and creative problem-solving.

Steve Kreiser, CDR (USN Ret.), MBA, is a Partner with Press Ganey Strategic Consulting. Steve has more than 30 years of experience improving safety and reliability in naval operations, military and commercial aviation, and healthcare. During his tenure with Press Ganey and Healthcare Performance Improvement (HPI), he has worked with more than 100 hospitals to improve patient safety, safety culture, leadership, cause analysis, and peer review.

Prior to joining HPI, Steve was an officer and F/A-18 pilot, retiring as a naval commander in 2008. During his naval career, he accumulated 3,500 flight hours and 720 carrier landings, including combat missions in Iraq, Bosnia, and Afghanistan. He also held positions designed to improve reliability and safety in naval aviation, serving on aircraft mishap investigation boards and human factors councils tasked with discovering root causes for aviation accidents and associated human errors.

Additionally, Steve has a unique background and perspective on team training from his commercial airline experience as a first officer with United Airlines where he worked extensively in the area of crew resource management. Steve holds a master of business administration degree from the University of Maryland University College and a bachelor of science degree in aerospace engineering from the University of Virginia.

Kristopher H. Morgan, PhD, is the Director of Workforce Analytics at Press Ganey. He has over 15 years of academic and professional research experience and is a nationally recognized leader in patient experience and engagement research. He is responsible for new-product development, metric creation, and maintaining Press Ganey's methodological processes and standards. His team developed a new Resilience Metric which is designed to combat burnout among physicians and frontline staff.

Kris frequently lectures on engagement and patient experience data and analytic strategies and has been published widely in academic and industry journals. His most recent publication, "The Relationship Between Nurse-Reported Safety Culture and the Patient Experience," appeared in the *Journal of Nursing Administration*. Kris has served as an adjunct professor at Indiana University South Bend, New Mexico State University, and Hillsdale College.

Deirdre E. Mylod, PhD, is the Executive Director of Press Ganey's Institute for Innovation and Senior Vice President of Research and Analytics. In this joint role, she is responsible for advancing the understanding of the entire patient experience, including patient satisfaction, clinical process, and outcomes. Through the institute, Deirdre partners with leading healthcare providers to study and implement transformative concepts for improving the patient experience.

Throughout her time at Press Ganey, Deirdre has served in a variety of key leadership roles. Most recently, she served as the vice president of Improvement Services, during which she oversaw the organization's Client Improvement Management teams. These teams offer clients quality-improvement strategy and solutions to enhance their performance in patient evaluations of care. Previously, she was responsible for developing Press Ganey's HCAHPS initiative and managing clients' participation in state-reporting projects. Deirdre served as Press Ganey's liaison to the National Quality Forum (NQF) and has served on committees on public reporting and consumer engagement through the NQF. Deirdre holds a master's degree and a doctoral degree in psychology from the University of Notre Dame.

Brad Pollins, MS, SPHR, is a Manager in the Transformational Services group at Press Ganey. He has more than three decades of professional experience in organizational development, strategic planning, change management, culture transformation, employee engagement, and leadership talent development.

Brad has worked in a variety of industries, including consulting, manufacturing, consumer products, utilities, insurance, telecommunications, and food service. For the past 20 years, Brad has worked in healthcare, where he has led programs to transform organizational culture to achieve better strategic and operational outcomes. He has been a key member of corporate leadership teams and has led several groundbreaking initiatives, including assessment centers, talent selection, discovery charts, Lean production, and leadership fellowships and academies. He built and led the organizational development function at Lee Health and authored *Awakening Your Organization: Performance Acceleration in Healthcare.*

Brad has received several recognitions including the President's Circle Award for Employee Engagement, and he helped lead people practices that resulted in achieving Employer of Choice and Premier Healthcare Employer awards for a large healthcare organization.

Brad holds a master's degree in industrial and organizational psychology and has been certified as a Florida Sterling Council and Malcolm Baldrige examiner.

David Shinsel leads the Workforce and Engagement Advisory team at Press Ganey. Since joining the company in 2012, David has held analytic, strategic, and consultative roles. In addition to his current role as a leader, David partners with healthcare systems across the nation to help them build excellence in engagement, safety, and patient experience through improving organizational culture.

David has authored strategic white papers, facilitated leader coaching and intensive workshops, and assisted in the development of technological solutions. David enjoys speaking on the topics of culture, safety, change management, and resilience, and is passionate about helping organizations translate data into action. He holds a master's degree in industrial/organizational psychology.

Ingrid Summers, MHS, joined Press Ganey as a Senior Associate in 2016, bringing more than two decades of experience in diversity and inclusion, organizational development, and talent management. As a Senior Associate, Ingrid is responsible for developing operational strategies to help caregivers across the nation improve the patient experience through the lens of diversity and inclusion, with an overarching goal of reducing the suffering of patients as they undergo care, thus improving the value of that care.

Prior to joining Press Ganey, Ingrid held leadership positions at several Fortune 100 companies, and she has led organizational development initiatives as both an internal and external consultant.

Matt Turner, MA, joined Press Ganey's Engagement Practice in 2013, bringing more than 20 years of operational and consulting experience to his role. As a trusted advisor to clients, he is an expert in the areas of organization development, strategy, and culture within healthcare settings, with a particular interest in leadership, talent management, and physician engagement. He is adept at distilling, synthesizing, and explaining complex data and helping clients develop effective improvement strategies. Matt has worked closely with many Press Ganey clients on their employee and physician engagement efforts, including Methodist Le Bonheur Healthcare, The University of Virginia Health System, Seattle Children's Hospital, Intermountain Healthcare, Providence St. Joseph Health, and UNC Healthcare, among others.

Prior to joining Press Ganey, Matt was assistant vice president for Leadership & Organizational Development at Carolinas HealthCare System (now Atrium Health) where he led a team responsible for executive and physician leadership development, physician governance, patient relationship management, and marketing. The medical group he supported included more than 1,300 physicians and advanced practitioners serving patients in over 300 locations across the Carolinas. Matt is a dynamic and experienced presenter, having made numerous presentations to physician groups and professional associations. He has been an invited speaker at the American Medical Group Association National Conference and the Medical Group Management Association National Conference.

Shannon Vincent is a Senior Associate with Press Ganey, bringing 15 years of experience advising healthcare organizations in implementing strategies that drive cultural transformation. Shannon has a background in industrial/organizational psychology with a focus on organizational development, leadership, and employee engagement. At Press Ganey, she works with client organizations to develop and implement engagement surveys and utilize statistical analyses to interpret results and develop effective improvement strategies that enable and activate their most strategic asset: their people.

Shannon's client work has most recently expanded to include implementing and sustaining efforts around patient and workforce safety through the application of High Reliability science. Prior to joining Press Ganey in 2016, Shannon advised client organizations in a variety of industries, including gaming, financial services, energy, and retail, to solve for workforce and leadership challenges.

Stephanie B. Weimer, MA, joined Press Ganey in 2014 as an Advisor on the Workforce Solutions team. Stephanie is responsible for providing guidance, leadership, training, and expertise in the creation and implementation of employee and physician engagement and culture initiatives. She brings a strong background of quantitative and qualitative research, statistical analysis, and survey design to her practice of helping organizations measure and improve engagement. She has experience training, coaching, and facilitating groups of all sizes, and has delivered presentations and workshops for hundreds of managers and executives. Moreover, she is a subject matter expert in advanced engagement analytics and helps organizations conduct analyses to provide additional insight into their culture and assist them with targeting action planning opportunities. She partners with a variety of healthcare organizations globally, including large integrated systems and academic medical centers.

Before joining Press Ganey, Stephanie taught an upper-level undergraduate research and statistics lab at Wake Forest University. Additionally, she has conducted experimental research in social cognition including attitude change, counterfactual thinking, and decision-making and has presented her research at American Psychological Association (APA) conferences. Stephanie holds a bachelor of arts degree in psychology from UNC Chapel Hill and a master of arts degree in psychology from Wake Forest University.

About the Editors

Joseph Cabral, MS, is the Chief Human Resources Officer and President of Workforce Solutions at Press Ganey, a position to which he brings significant experience driving cultural transformation and caregiver engagement to support Press Ganey's broad client base.

Most recently, Joe was chief human resources officer at Partners HealthCare, one of the largest diversified healthcare service organizations in the United States. With more than 20 years of experience developing and executing strategies that enhance cultural and organizational change, Joe has spent more than a decade driving business objectives, vision, and values forward in all aspects of talent management and human resources to achieve the organization's goals. Prior to Partners HealthCare, Joe served as chief human resources officer at Cleveland Clinic and at Northwell Health, and he has held key HR leadership roles at NewYork–Presbyterian Hospital and Boston Children's Hospital.

Joe holds a master's degree in quality systems management, has taught as an adjunct professor at the University of Massachusetts, and has served as a Baldrige examiner as well as on New York's Regional Economic Development Council. He has been cited by *Time*, *BusinessWeek*, *The Wall Street Journal*, the *New York Times*, *Forbes*, and other industry publications for his expertise in human resources best practices, and in 2014 he received the CHRO of the Year Award from HRO Today.

Thomas H. Lee, MD, MSc, joined Press Ganey as Chief Medical Officer in 2013, bringing more than three decades of experience in healthcare performance improvement as a practicing physician, leader in provider organizations, researcher, and health policy expert. As CMO, Tom is responsible for developing clinical and operational strategies to help providers across the nation measure and improve the patient experience, with an overarching goal of reducing the suffering of patients as they undergo care and improving the value of that care. In addition to his role with Press Ganey, Tom, an internist and cardiologist, continues to practice primary care at Brigham and Women's Hospital in Boston.

Tom frequently lectures on the patient experience and strategies for improving the value of healthcare and was selected as a stage speaker on the subject at the acclaimed TEDMED meeting in 2015. He has authored more than 260 academic articles and the books *Chaos and Organization in Health Care* and *Eugene Braunwald and the Rise of Modern Medicine*. In November 2015, Tom released his third book, *An Epidemic of Empathy in Healthcare: How to Deliver Compassionate, Connected Patient Care That Creates a Competitive Advantage*, published by McGraw-Hill.

In November 2019, he released his fourth book, *The Good Doctor: What It Means, How to Become One, and How to Remain One*, also published by McGraw-Hill.

Martin Wright is a Partner in Press Ganey's Transformational Advisory Services group. In this role, he is responsible for supporting Press Ganey's Advisory Services and Transformational Solutions practices, focused on advancing the caregiver experience and delivering workforce solutions to enhance organizational culture, including safety culture and employee and physician engagement.

Marty has 17 years of experience working in healthcare market research, process improvement, and patient safety. As a consultant, he has helped hundreds of client organizations, ranging from small critical access hospitals to large integrated health systems, improve patient, employee, and provider experiences. As a leader, he has developed his teams to ensure that the right data are captured, reported, and analyzed to meet each organization's unique needs. Currently, he leads a team of 23 solutions experts who partner with healthcare leaders to provide actionable insights aimed at developing and retaining high-performing staff and building patient loyalty.

Marty has been a featured speaker at many national healthcare conferences and has authored several articles for prominent healthcare publications. He holds a bachelor of arts degree from Purdue University.

About Press Ganey

PRESS GANEY WAS founded more than 30 years ago, based on a passion to help improve the way in which healthcare is delivered. Today, that principle remains a core element of Press Ganey's mission to help healthcare organizations across the continuum reduce suffering and enhance caregiver resilience to improve the safety, quality, and experience of care.

Press Ganey partners with providers to capture the voices of patients, physicians, nurses, and employees to gain insights to address unmet needs. Through the use of integrated data, advanced analytics, and strategic advisory services, Press Ganey helps clients transform their organizations to deliver safer, high-quality, patient- and family-centered care.

Press Ganey is recognized as a pioneer and thought leader in patient experience measurement and performance improvement solutions. As a strategic business partner to more than 26,000 healthcare organizations, Press Ganey leads the industry in helping clients transform the patient experience and create continuous sustainable improvement to healthcare delivery.

For more information, please visit pressganey.com.

Also from Press Ganey

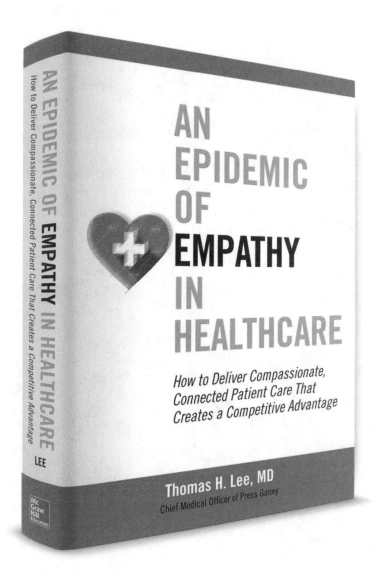

AN EPIDEMIC OF EMPATHY IN HEALTHCARE

How to Deliver Compassionate, Connected Patient Care That Creates a Competitive Advantage

Thomas H. Lee, MD
Chief Medical Officer of Press Ganey

978-1259583018

Also from Press Ganey

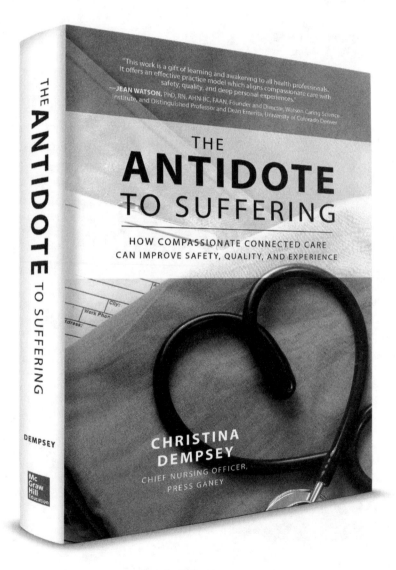

978-1260116557

Also from Press Ganey

"A turning point in patient safety, this book will unleash the power and talent of health systems in pursuit of transformative safety and experience."
—A. MARC HARRISON, MD, President and CEO, Intermountain Healthcare

ZER HARM

HOW TO ACHIEVE PATIENT AND WORKFORCE SAFETY IN HEALTHCARE

Edited by
Craig Clapper, PE
James Merlino, MD
Carole Stockmeier
of Press Ganey

978-1260440928

Also from Press Ganey

978-1259583018